RACE QUESTIONS, PROVINCIALISM
AND OTHER AMERICAN PROBLEMS

RACE QUESTIONS

PROVINCIALISM

AND OTHER AMERICAN PROBLEMS

BY

JOSIAH ROYCE

PROFESSOR OF THE HISTORY OF PHILOSOPHY
IN HARVARD UNIVERSITY

Essay Index Reprint Series

BOOKS FOR LIBRARIES PRESS
FREEPORT, NEW YORK

INTERNATIONAL STANDARD BOOK NUMBER:

0-8369-0842-2

LIBRARY OF CONGRESS CATALOG CARD NUMBER:

67-23266

PRINTED IN THE UNITED STATES OF AMERICA

PREFACE

THE five essays which make up the present volume were all, at some time, read, before various audiences, as addresses. Each one contains indications of the special occasion for the sake of which it was first prepared. Yet each one of them also states opinions which, from my own point of view, make it a part of an effort to apply, to some of our American problems, that general doctrine about life which I have recently summed up in my book entitled "The Philosophy of Loyalty." In the light of that philosophy I therefore hope that the various special opinions here expressed may be judged. This book I regard as an auxiliary to its more systematic predecessor.

The closing essay of the present volume contains, in fact, a summary of the theses upon which my "Philosophy of Loyalty" is based, as well as a direct application of these theses to a special practical problem of our recent education.

The first essay here printed — that on " Race Questions " — was read before the Chicago Ethical Society, in 1905. It was later published in the " International Journal of Ethics." It is an effort to express and to justify, in the special case of the race-problems, the spirit which I have elsewhere defined as that of " Loyalty to Loyalty."

The second and fourth essays of this book both relate to " Provincialism," — the one discussing, in general terms, the need and uses of that spirit in our American life ; the other sketching, as well as I am able, the bases upon which rests that particular form of provincialism to which I, as a native Californian, personally owe most. The paper on " The Pacific Coast " was prepared as early as 1898. The general essay on " Provincialism " was read as a Phi Beta Kappa Address, at the Iowa State University, in 1902. In the " Philosophy of Loyalty " the importance of an enlightened provincialism is discussed in the course of the fifth lecture of that volume, — a lecture whose general topic is: "Certain American Problems in their Relation to Loyalty." What I there merely sketched regarding provincialism is here more fully set forth. In my own mind, meanwhile, the essay on the "Pacific Coast" is a continuation of the study which first took form in my volume on the history of California, published, in the Commonwealth Series, in 1886. In that work I stated, in various passages, views about the provincial aspects of loyalty, — views which have later come to form part of the more general ethical doctrine to which I am now committed.

Loyalty is the practical aspect and expression of an idealistic philosophy. Such a philosophy, in relation to theoretical as well as to practical problems, I have long tried to maintain and to teach. A familiar charge against idealism, however, is, that it is an essentially unpractical doctrine. Such a charge can be fairly answered only in case an idealist is quite willing, not only to listen with good humor to his common-sense critics, but also to criticise himself and to observe the defects of his tendencies. In such a spirit I have tried to write the third of the essays here printed. I should be glad to have this paper read in the light of the lecture on "Conscience," in the "Philosophy of Loyalty."

Some passages in these papers show special signs of the dates when they were written; and therefore the reader may notice a few allusions and illustrations — due to passing events — which would be otherwise chosen or stated were the papers composed to-day. Thus, my sketch of conditions in Jamaica, in the essay on "Race Questions," contains a few s atistical and other data that were publicly reported in 1904, and that would need some modification to adapt them to the present moment. But I believe that none of these matters interfere with what my volume attempts to be, — a series of illustrations, prepared in the course of a number of years, but all bearing upon the application of a certain philosophical doctrine and spirit to some problems of American life.

I have mentioned the Japanese, more than once, in these pages. It is fair to say that the characterization of their national spirit which occurs in the essay on " Provincialism " was written in 1902, and here appears substantially unchanged.

Mrs. Royce has constantly aided me in preparing these essays for publication; and to her help many things in this volume are due.

JOSIAH ROYCE.

CAMBRIDGE, MASS.,
October 16, 1908.

CONTENTS

xi

CONTENTS

CONTENTS

I

RACE QUESTIONS AND PREJUDICES

I

RACE QUESTIONS AND PREJUDICES

THE numerous questions and prejudices which are aroused by the contact of the various races of men have always been important factors in human history. They promise, however, to become, in the near future, still more important than they have ever been before. Such increased importance of race questions and prejudices, if it comes to pass, will be due not to any change in human nature, and especially not to any increase in the diversity or in the contrasting traits of the races of men themselves, but simply to the greater extent and complexity of the work of civilization. Physically speaking, great masses of men are to-day brought into more frequent and closer contact than was formerly possible, because of the ease with which at present the numerous means of communication can be used, because of the increase of peaceful migrations, and because of the imperial ambitions of several of the world's great peoples. Hence whatever contact, conflict, or mutual influence the races of men have had in the past, we find to-day more ways and places in which men find themselves in the presence of alien races, with whom they have to learn to live in the same social order. When we think of East Indian coolies now present as laborers, side by side with the native negroes, and with white men, in the British West Indies; when we remember the problem of South Africa, as it was impressed upon our minds a few years since, at a moment when Dutchmen and Englishmen fought for the land, while Kaffirs and Zulus watched the conflict; when we recall what the recent war between Japan and Russia has already meant for the future of the races of men in the far East; and when, with a few only of such typical instances in mind, we turn back to our own country, and think how many different race-problems confront us, — we then see that the earliest social problem of humanity is also the most recent problem. This is the problem of dealing with the men who seem to us somehow very widely different from ourselves, in physical constitution, in temperament, in all their deeper nature, so that we are tempted to think of them as natural strangers to our souls, while nevertheless we find that they are stubbornly there in our world, and that they are men as much determined to live as we are, and are men who, in turn, find us as incomprehensible as we find them. Of these diverse races, what ones are the superior and what ones are the inferior races? What race or races ought to rule? What ones ought to yield to their natural masters? To which one of these races has God, or nature, or destiny, ordained the rightful and final sovereignty of the earth? Which of these types of men is really the human type? Are they by their presence and their rivalry essentially perilous to one another's interests? And if so, what one amongst them is there whose spread, or whose increase in power or in number, is most perilous to the true cause of civilization? Is it a "yellow peril," or a "black peril," or perhaps, after all, is it not rather some form of "white peril," which most threatens the future of humanity in this day of great struggles and of complex issues? Are all men equal, as the Eighteenth Century theorists insisted? Or if the actual inequality of men in power, in value, in progressiveness, is an obvious fact, then how is this fact related to racial distinctions?

Such are a few of the questions that crowd upon us when we think about the races of men, and about their various relations to civilization. I do not mean, in this brief discussion, to exhaust any of these questions, but I want to call attention to a few principles which seem to me to be serviceable to any one who wants to look at race questions fairly and humanely.

I

It will be natural for some of my readers to interpose, at this point, the suggestion that the principal guidance in any attempt to answer such questions as the foregoing must

come from an appeal to the results of the
modern scientific study of the races of men.
Why speculate and moralize, one may say?
Have not the races of men been studied in
recent times with elaborate care? What can
tell us how to deal with the race-problems,
in case we neglect the results of anthropology
and of ethnology? And if we consult those
sciences, do they not already give us a basis
for decision regarding all such matters — a
basis which is far more valuable than any
chance observations of an amateur can be?

As a fact, if I supposed that, in their present stage of progress, the sciences which
deal with man had already attained to exact
results regarding the mental and moral differences, prospects, and destinies, of the different stocks of the *genus homo*, nobody would
be humbler than I should be in accepting,
and in trying to use the verdict that would
then have been obtained. But I confess
that, as a student of ethics and of certain other
aspects of our common human nature, I have
been a good deal baffled in trying to discover

just what the results of science are regarding the true psychological and moral meaning of race-differences. I shall later speak further of some of the difficulties of this scientific aspect of our topic. It is enough to say here that when I consult any of the known *Rassentheoretiker* for light, I do indeed learn that the concept of race is the key to the comprehension of all history, and that, if you only form a clear idea of the important types of men (types such, for instance, as the marvellous *Germanen* of Chamberlain's *Grundzüge des Neunzehnten Jahrhunderts*), you can then determine with exactness precisely who ought to rule and who ought to yield, and can predict the forms of civilization, the *Weltanschauungen,* and the other possessions, which will be characteristic of each type of men, so long as that type shall endure. When I observe, however, that the *Rassentheoretiker* frequently uses his science to support most of his personal prejudices, and is praised by his sympathizers almost equally for his exact knowledge and for his vigorous display of temperament, I begin to wonder whether a science which mainly devotes itself to proving that we ourselves are the salt of the earth, is after all so exact as it aims to be. It is with some modern race-theories, as it is with some forms of international yacht racing. I know nothing about yachting; but whenever any form of the exalted sport of international yachting proves to be definable as a sort of contest in which the foreigner is invariably beaten, I for my part take no interest in learning more about the rules of that particular game. And precisely so, when men marshal all the resources of their science to prove that their own race-prejudices are infallible, I can feel no confidence in what they imagine to be the result of science. Much of our modern race-theory reminds me, in its spirit, altogether too much of some of the conversations in the "Jungle Book," — or of the type of international courtesy expressed in "The Truce of the Bear," — too much, I say to seem like exact science. Mowgli's remarks addressed to Red

Dog may have been good natural history; but scientific Zoölogy does not proceed in that way.

While I deeply respect, then, the actual work of the sciences which deal with man, and while I fully recognize their modern progress, I greatly doubt that these sciences as yet furnish us with the exact results which representative race-theorists sometimes insist upon. Hence I am unable to begin this little study by a mere report of what science has established regarding the mental and moral varieties of men. I must rather make my beginning with a mention of two instances which have recently been much in my mind, and which bear upon the meaning of race prejudices. One of these instances is to-day in everybody's mind.

II

I refer then, first, to the wonderful lesson that Japan has been teaching us regarding what human energy and devotion have done and can do, and can do also in case of a race that is indeed remote enough from our own.

I remember well the Japan of the geography text-books of my childhood, text-books which were even then antiquated enough; but I believed them. Japan was a weird land, according to the old text-books, — a land from which foreigners were excluded, a land where all things were as perverse as possible, where criminals were boiled in oil, where Catholic missionaries had long ago been martyred. Whatever the Japanese were, they were plainly men of the wrong race. Later, however, I learned something of the contemporary history of Japan as it then was. The scene was now, indeed, vastly changed. The Japanese had opened their land; and hereupon, lo! in a magic way, they were imitating, so we heard, *all* of our European customs. So we next had to alter our own opinion as to their essential nature. They became in our eyes a plastic race of wonderful little children, small of stature, quick of wit, light-minded — a folk who took up any suggestion precisely as the playful children often do. They, too, were playing, it seemed, with our whole

Western civilization. Plainly, then, they were a race who had no serious life of their own at all. Those of us who disliked them noted that they thus showed an ape-like unsteadiness of conduct. This, then, was their racial characteristic. Those who admired them thought of them as a new sort of pets, to be humored and instructed with all our superior condescension. Well, as time went on, and I grew to manhood, I myself came to know some of these Japanese as students. Hereupon, however, I gradually learned to see such men in a wholly new light. I found them, with all their steadfast courtesy, pleasantly, but impenetrably reserved — keepers of their own counsel, men whose life had, as I soon found, a vast background of opinions and customs that I could not fathom. When, I said, shall I ever see what is behind that Japanese smile? What is in their hearts? With an immovable self-consciousness they resisted every effort to alter, from without, any of their essential ideals. Politely, whenever you pressed them, they declined to admit that any of our Western arts or opinions were equal in value to their own most cherished national ideal treasures. And this they did even at the moment when they were present, most respectfully, as learners. They learned well; but plainly they meant to use this learning for their own purposes. An enthusiastic lady in an American University town was once seeking to draw from a Japanese visitor some admission of the importance of Christianity for the higher civilization of his country. "Confess," she insisted, "confess what a boon our missionaries have brought you in introducing Christianity into your land." "You are right," answered the Japanese, with his usual courteous smile, "you are right; the missionaries in introducing Christianity, have indeed brought us a great good. They have completed the variety of religions in Japan."

This impenetrable Japanese self-consciousness, this unconquerable polite and obstinate reserve, what did it mean? Well, Mr. Hearn and his kin have now let us know in a literary way something of the true heart of Japan.

13

And the recent war has shown us what Japan meant by imitating our Western ways, and also what ancestral ideals have led her sons to death in battle, and still hold the nation so closely knit to their Emperor. Already I have heard some tender souls amongst us say: "It is *they* who are racially *our* superiors." Some of us may live to see Japanese customs pervading our land, and all of our professional imitators trying to be Japanese.

Well, I myself am no worshipper of any new fancy or distant civilization, merely because of its temporary prominence. But the true lesson which Japan teaches us to-day is, that it is somewhat hard to find out by looking at the features of a man's face, or at the color of his skin, or even at the reports of travellers who visit his land, what it is of which his race is really capable. Perhaps the Japanese are not of the right race; but we now admit that so long as we judged them merely by their race, and by mere appearances, we were judging them ignorantly, and falsely. This, I say, has been to me a most interesting lesson in the fallibility of some of our race judgments.

III

So much, then, for one lesson of experience. I have recently been much impressed by another lesson, but by one of a very different character, occurring, so to speak, at the other extremity of the world of modern race-problems. The negro has so far shown none of the great powers of the Japanese. Let us, then, provisionally admit at this stage of our discussion that the negro is in his present backward state as a race, for reasons which are not due merely to circumstances, but which are quite innate in his mental constitution. I shall indeed return to that topic later on. But, for the moment, let that view pass as if it were finally accepted. View the negro, then, for the instant merely as a backward race. But let the race-question here be our own pressing Southern question: How can the white man and the negro, once forced, as they are in our South, to live side by side, best learn to live with a minimum of friction, with a maximum of coöperation? I have long learned from my Southern friends that this end can only be attained by a firm and by a very constant and explicit insistence upon keeping the negro in his proper place, as a social inferior — who, then, as an inferior, should, of course, be treated humanely, but who must first be clearly and unmistakably taught where he belongs. I have observed that the pedagogical methods which my Southern friends of late years have found it their duty to use, to this end, are methods such as still keep awake a good deal of very lively and intense irritation in the minds not only of the pupils but also of the teachers. Now irritation, viewed merely in itself, is not an enlightening state of mind. It is, therefore, according to our modern views, not a very pedagogical state of mind. I am myself, for instance, a fairly irritable person, and I am also a teacher. But at the moments when I am irritated I am certainly not just then a good teacher. Is, however, the irritation which seems to be

the accompaniment of some of the recent
Southern methods of teaching the negro his
place an inevitable evil, a wholly necessary
accompaniment of the present transition period
in the South? *Must* such increase of race-
hatred first come, in order that later, whenever the negro has fully learned his lesson,
and aspires no more beyond his station, peace
may come? Well, concerning just this matter I lately learned what was to me, in
my inexperience, a new lesson. I have had
occasion three times, in recent summers,
to visit British West Indies, Jamaica, and
Trinidad, at a time when few tourists were
there. Upon visiting Jamaica I first went
round the coast of the island, visiting its
various ports. I then went inland, and walked
for miles over its admirable country roads.
I discussed its condition with men of various
occupations. I read some of its official literature. I then consulted with a new interest its
history. I watched its negroes in various
places, and talked with some of them, too.
I have since collected such further informa-

tion as I had time to collect regarding its life, as various authorities have discussed the topic, and this is the result: —

Jamaica has a population of surely not more than 14,000 or 15,000 whites, mostly English. Its black population considerably exceeds 600,000. Its mulatto population, of various shades, numbers, at the very least, some 40,000 or 50,000. Its plantation life, in the days before emancipation, was much sadder and severer, by common account, than ours in the South ever was. Both the period of emancipation and the immediately following period were of a very discouraging type. In the sixties of the last century there was one very unfortunate insurrection. The economic history of the island has also been in many ways unlucky even to the present day. Here, then, are certainly conditions which in some respects are decidedly such as would seem to tend toward a lasting state of general irritation, such as you might suppose would make race-questions acute. Moreover, the population, being a tropical one, has serious moral burdens to contend with of the sort that result from the known influences of such climates upon human character in the men of all races.

And yet, despite all these disadvantages, to-day, whatever the problems of Jamaica, whatever its defects, our own present Southern race-problem in the forms which we know best, simply does not exist. There is no public controversy about social race equality or superiority. Neither a white man nor a white woman feels insecure in moving about freely amongst the black population anywhere on the island. The colony has a Legislative Assembly, although one of extremely limited legislative powers. For the choice to this assembly a suffrage determined only by a decidedly low rate-qualification is free to all who have sufficient property, but is used by only a very small portion of the negro population. The negro is, on the whole, neither painfully obstrusive in his public manners, nor in need of being sharply kept in his place. Within the circles of the black population itself there is meanwhile a decidedly rich social differentiation. There are negroes in government service, negroes in the professions, negroes who are fairly prosperous peasant proprietors, and there are also the poor peasants; there are the thriftless, the poor in the towns, — yes, as in any tropical country, the beggars. In Kingston and in some other towns there is a small class of negroes who are distinctly criminal. On the whole, however, the negroes and colored population, taken in the mass, are orderly, law-abiding, contented, still backward in their education, but apparently advancing. They are generally loyal to the government. The best of them are aspiring, in their own way, and wholesomely self-conscious. Yet there is no doubt whatever that English white men are the essential controllers of the destiny of the country. But these English whites, few as they are, control the country at present, with extraordinarily little friction, and wholly without those painful emotions, those insistent complaints and anxieties, which at present are so prominent in the minds of many of our own Southern brethren. Life in Jamaica is not ideal. The economical aspect of the island is in many ways unsatisfactory. But the negro race-question, in our present American sense of that term, seems to be substantially solved.

How? By race-mixture?

The considerable extent to which race-mixture went in the earlier history of Jamaica is generally known. Here, as elsewhere, however, it has been rather the social inequality of the races, than any approach to equality, which has been responsible for the mixture, in so far as such has occurred. It was the social inequality of the plantation days that began the process of mixture. If the often-mentioned desire to raise the "color" of their children, has later led the colored population to seek a further amalgamation of the two stocks, certainly that tendency, so far as it is effective, has been due to the social advantages of the lighter color — and not due to any motive which has decreased the ancient disadvantages under which the darker race has had to suffer. If race-amalgamation is indeed to be viewed as always an evil, the best way to counteract the growth of that evil must everywhere be the cultivation of racial self-respect and not of racial degradation. As a fact, it is not the amalgamation of the stocks, so far as that has occurred, which has tended to reduce the friction between the races in Jamaica. As to the English newcomers to the island, they probably do not tend to become amalgamated with the colored stocks in Jamaica, more than in any other region where the English live. The English stock tends, here as elsewhere, to be proud of itself, and to keep to itself. How then has the solution of what was once indeed a grave race-question been brought about in Jamaica?

I answer, by the simplest means in the world — the simplest, that is, for Englishmen — viz.: by English administration, and by English reticence. When once the sad period of emancipation and of subsequent occasional disorder was passed, the Englishman did in

Jamaica what he has so often and so well done elsewhere. He organized his colony; he established good local courts, which gained by square treatment the confidence of the blacks. The judges of such courts were Englishmen. The English ruler also provided a good country constabulary, in which native blacks also found service, and in which they could exercise authority over other blacks. Black men, in other words, were trained, under English management, of course, to police black men. A sound civil service was also organized; and in that educated negroes found in due time their place, while the chiefs of each branch of the service were and are, in the main, Englishmen. The excise and the health services, both of which are very highly developed, have brought the law near to the life of the humblest negro, in ways which he sometimes finds, of course, restraining, but which he also frequently finds beneficent. Hence he is accustomed to the law; he sees its ministers often, and often, too, as men of his own race; and in the main, he is fond of

23

order, and learns to be respectful toward the established ways of society. The Jamaica negro is described by those who know him as especially fond of bringing his petty quarrels and personal grievances into court. He is litigious just as he is vivacious. But this confidence in the law is just what the courts have encouraged. That is one way, in fact, to deal with the too forward and strident negro. Encourage him to air his grievances in court, listen to him patiently, and fine him when he deserves fines. That is a truly English type of social pedagogy. It works in the direction of making the negro a conscious helper toward good social order.

Administration, I say, has done the larger half of the work of solving Jamaica's race-problem. Administration has filled the island with good roads, has reduced to a minimum the tropical diseases by means of an excellent health-service, has taught the population loyalty and order, has led them some steps already on the long road "up from slavery," has given them, in many cases, the true self-respect of those who themselves officially co-operate in the work of the law, and it has done this without any such result as our Southern friends nowadays conceive when they think of what is called "negro domination." Administration has allayed ancient irritations. It has gone far to offset the serious economic and tropical troubles from which Jamaica meanwhile suffers.

Yes, the work has been done by administration, — and by reticence. For the Englishman, in his official and governmental dealings with backward peoples, has a great way of being superior without very often publicly saying that he is superior. You well know that in dealing, as an individual, with other individuals, trouble is seldom made by the fact that you are actually the superior of another man in any respect. The trouble comes when you tell the other man, too stridently, that you are his superior. Be my superior, quietly, simply showing your superiority in your deeds, and very likely I shall love you for the very fact of your superiority.

For we all love our leaders. But tell me that I am your inferior, and then perhaps I may grow boyish, and may throw stones. Well, it is so with races. Grant then that yours is the superior race. Then you can afford to say little about that subject in your public dealings with the backward race. Superiority is best shown by good deeds and by few boasts.

IV

So much for the lesson that Jamaica has suggested to me. The widely different conditions of Trinidad suggest, despite the differences, a somewhat similar lesson. Here also there are great defects in the social order; but again, our Southern race-problem does not exist. When, with such lessons in mind, I recall our problem, as I hear it from my brethren of certain regions of our Union, I see how easily we can all mistake for a permanent race-problem a difficulty that is essentially a problem of quite another sort. Mr. Thomas Nelson Page in his recent book on the "Southerners' Problem" speaks,

in one notable passage, of the possibility which
he calls Utopian, that perhaps some day the
negro in the South may be made to coöperate
in the keeping of order by the organization
under State control of a police of his own
race, who shall deal with blacks. He even
mentions that the English in the East Indies
use native constabulary. But this possibility
is not Utopian. When I hear the complaint
of the Southerner, that the race-problem
is such as constantly to endanger the safety
of his home, I now feel disposed to say: "The
problem that endangers the sanctity of your
homes and that is said sometimes to make
lynching a necessity, is not a race-problem.
It is an administrative problem. You have
never organized a country constabulary.
Hence, when various social conditions, amongst
which the habit of irritating public speech
about race-questions is indeed one, though
only one, condition, have tended to the pro-
ducing and to the arousing of extremely
dangerous criminals in your communities,
you have no adequate means of guarding

27

against the danger. When you complain that such criminals, when they flee from justice, get sympathy from some portion of their ignorant fellows and so are aided to get away, you forget that you have not first made your negro countryman familiar with, and fond of, the law, by means of a vigorous and well-organized and generally beneficent administration constantly before his eyes, not only in the pursuit of criminals, but in the whole care of public order and health. If you insist that in some districts the white population is too sparse or too poor, or both, to furnish an efficient country constabulary constantly on duty, why, then, have you not long since trained black men to police black men? Sympathy with the law grows with responsibility for its administration. If it is revolting to you to see black men possessed of the authority of a country constabulary, still, if you will, you can limit their authority to a control over their own race. If you say all this speech of mine is professorial, unpractical, Utopian, and if you still cry out bitterly for the effective protection of your womankind, I reply merely, look at Jamaica. Look at other English colonies.

In any case, the Southern race-problem will never be relieved by speech or by practices such as increase irritation. It will be relieved when administration grows sufficiently effective, and when the negroes themselves get an increasingly responsible part in this administration in so far as it relates to their own race. That may seem a wild scheme. But I insist: It is the English way. Look at Jamaica, and learn how to protect your own homes.

I have reviewed two very different lessons which I have recently had brought home to me regarding race-problems. What is there which is common to these two lessons? Is it not this: In estimating, in dealing with races, in defining what their supposedly unchangeable characteristics are, in planning what to do with them, we are all prone to confuse the accidental with the essential. We are likely to take for an essential race-characteristic what is a transient incident, or a product of special social conditions. We are disposed to view as a fatal and overwhelming race-problem what is a perfectly curable accident of our present form of administration. If we are indeed of a superior race ourselves, we shall, however, best prove the fact by learning to distinguish the accidental from the essential in our relations with other races. I speak with no lack of sympathy for the genuine and bitter trials of our Southern brethren when I say that I suppose the mistake which I now point out, the mistake of confusing the essential and the accidental, is the mistake that they are now making in many of their sincerest expressions of concern over their race-problem.

So much for the two lessons that have led me to the present discussion. But now let me pass to a somewhat wider view of race-problems. Let me ask a little more generally, What, if anything, can be known to be essential about the characteristics of a race of men and consequently an essentially important consideration in our dealings with alien races? Speaking so far as we can, apart from prejudice, what can we say about what it is which distinguishes the various races of men from one another?

V

The term "race" is popularly used in a very vague way. The newspapers not long ago said, during trouble in Poland, that the Russian soldiers then in Warsaw showed "race-antipathy" in their conflicts with the people. We all know, however, that the mutual hatred of Russians and Poles is due mainly to political and to religious causes. Frenchmen of the northern provinces, who are anthropologically wholly indistinguishable, as Professor Ripley tells us, from the inhabitants of many western German districts, still have what they call a "race-antipathy" for the men across the border. Thus almost any national or political or religious barrier, if it is old enough, may lead to a consciousness of difference of race. On the other hand, there are, of course, unquestionable physical varieties of mankind, distinguished by well-known physical contrasts.

31

But the anthropologists still almost hopelessly disagree as to what the accurate classification of these true races may be. Such a classification, however, does not concern us here. We are now interested in the minds of men. We want to know what the races of men are socially good for. And not in the study of skulls or of hair, or of skin color, and not in the survey of all these bewildering complications with which physical anthropology deals, shall we easily find an answer to our more practical questions, viz., to our questions regarding the way in which these various races of men are related to the interests of civilization, and regarding the spirit in which we ought to estimate and practically to deal with these racial traits of mankind.

For after all, it is a man's mind, rather than his skull, or his hair, or his skin, that we most need to estimate. And if hereupon we ask ourselves just how these physical varieties of the human stock, just how these shades of color, these types of hair, these forms of skull, or these contours of body, are related to the

mental powers and to the moral characteristics of the men in question, then, if only we
set prejudice wholly aside, and appeal to
science to help us, we find ourselves in the
present state of knowledge almost hopelessly
at sea. We know too little as yet about the
natural history of the human mind, our psychology is far too infantile a science, to give
us any precise information as to the way in
which the inherited, the native, the constitu-
tional aspects of the minds of men really vary
with their complexions or with their hair.
Yet that, of course, is just what we most want
to know. It is easy to show that an Australian is just now far below our mental level.
But how far is his degradation due to the inherited and unchangeable characters of his
race, and how far to his long struggle with
the dreary desert? How far is he, as we now
find him, a degenerate, whose ancestors were
on some far higher level? In other words,
is his type of mind a true variety of the human
mind, inbred and unchangeable? How far
is it, so to speak, a mere incident? Upon

what level were the minds of our own ancestors in the early stone age of Europe? How
did their minds then compare with the minds
of those ancestors of the Australian who were
then their contemporaries? Who shall answer such questions? Yet just such questions we should have to answer before we could
decide upon the true relations of race and of
mind.

To be sure, anthropology has made a
beginning, and a very important beginning,
in the study of the mental types of primitive
man. By various comparative and arch-
æological methods we can already learn a good
deal about the minds of our own ancestors.
We can also study various races as they are
to-day. We know, about the early stages of
human culture, far more than we knew a
little while since. But one result may forthwith be stated regarding what we have so far
learned concerning the early history of the
human mind, whether it is the mind of our
ancestors, or of other races. Of course, we
cannot doubt that, just as now we widely

differ in mental life, so always there must have been great contrasts between the minds of the various stocks of men. No doubt, if the science of man were exact, it would indeed include a race-psychology. But my present scepticism concerns the present state of science, and the result of such study as we have yet made of the racial psychology of man is distinctly disappointing to those who want to make their task easy by insisting that the physical varieties of mankind are in our present state of knowledge sufficient guides to an interpretation of the whole inner contrast of the characters and of the mental processes of men. For what anthropology thus far shows us is, that, so soon as you go back beyond those stages of cultivation where history is possible, and so soon as you view men as they are apart from the higher culture — well, then, all men, so far as we can yet study them, appear to us not, of course, the same in mind, but yet surprisingly alike in their minds, in their morals, and in their arts. Widely as the primitive men differ, in certain broad features they remain, for our present knowledge, notably similar. And these common features are such as are by no means altogether flattering to our racial pride, when we think that our own ancestors, too, were, not very long since, comparatively, primitive men like the rest.

All the more primitive men, namely, are largely alike in the grossness and in the unpromising stupidity of their superstitions, and in their moral defects and virtues. Very many of them, belonging to the most various races, resemble one another in possessing customs which we now, for the most part, profoundly abhor, and which we are at present prone to view as characteristic of essentially debased minds. Such customs as cannibalism, or as human sacrifice, or as the systematic torturing of prisoners of war, such horrors as those of the witchcraft from whose bondage Europeans escaped only since the seventeenth century — such things, I say, are characteristic of no one race of men. To surround one's life with a confused mass of spiritual horrors, to believe in ghosts, or in vampires, in demons, in magic, in witchcraft, and in hostile gods of all sorts, to tangle up one's daily activities in a net of superstitious customs, to waste time in elaborate incantations, to live in fantastic terrors of an unseen world, to be terrified by tabus of all kinds, so that numerous sorts of useful deeds are superstitiously forbidden, to narrate impossible stories and believe in them, to live in filth, to persecute, to resist light, to fight against progress, to be mentally slothful, dull, sensuous, cruel, to be the prey of endless foolishness, to be treacherous, to be destructive — well, these are the mental traits of no one or two races of men. These are simply the common evil, traits of primitive humanity, traits to which our own ancestors were very long ago a prey, traits against which civilized man has still constantly to fight. Any frenzied mob of civilized men may relapse in an hour to the level of a very base savagery. All the religions of men, without exception, and however lofty the heights that they have since climbed, appear to have begun with much the same chaos of weird customs and of unreasonable delusions. Man's mental burdens have thus been, in all races, of very much the same sort, except, to be sure, that civilization, side by side with the good that it has created, has invented some new mental burdens, such as our increasing percentage of insanity in recent times illustrates.

The souls of men, then, if viewed apart from the influences of culture, if viewed as they were in primitive times, are by no means as easy to classify as the woolly-haired and the straight-haired races at first appear to be. If you study the thoughts of the various peoples, as the anthropologist Bastian has loved to mass them together in his chaotic and learned monographs, or as Fraser has surveyed some of them in his " Golden Bough," well, these primitive thoughts appear, in all their own chaos, and in all their vast varieties of detail, to be the outcome not of racial differences so much as of a few essentially human, although by no means always very lofty, motives. These fundamental motives appear, with almost monotonous regularity, in the superstitions, the customs, the legends, of all races. Esquimaux and Australians, negroes and Scotch Highlanders of former days, ancient Japanese and Hindoos, Polynesians and early Greeks, — all these appear side by side, in such comparative studies of the primitive mind of man, side by side as brothers in error and in ignorance, so soon as you proceed to study by the comparative method their early magic, their old beliefs, their early customs. Yet only by such a study could you hope to distinguish what really belongs to the mind of a race of men, as distinct from what belongs to culture.

If, then, it is the mind and the heart of man that you really want to know, you will find it hard, so soon as you leave civilization out of account, to tell what the precise meaning of the term "race of men" is, when that term is conceived as characterizing a distinct hereditary variety of human mental constitution.

A race-psychology is still a science for the future to discover.

Perhaps, however, as you may say, I have not been just, in this very summary statement, to what, after all, may prove to be the best test of the true racial differences amongst the various types of the human mind. Some races, namely, have proved themselves to be *capable of civilization.* Other races have stubbornly refused civilization, or have remained helplessly degraded even when surrounded by civilization. Others still have perished at the first contact with civilization. The Germanic ancestors of the present western Europeans were barbarians, although of a high type. But when they met civilization, they first adopted, and then improved it. Not so was it with the Indians, with the Polynesians. Here, then, is the test of a true mental difference amongst races. Watch them when they meet civilization. Do they show themselves first teachable and then originative? Then they are mentally higher races. Do they stagnate or die out in the presence of civilization? Then they are of the lower types. Such differences, you will say, are deep and ineradicable, like the differences between the higher and the lower sorts of individual men. And such differences will enable us to define racial types of mind.

I fully agree that this test is an important one. Unfortunately, the test has never been so fairly applied by the civilized nations of men that it can give us any exact results. Again, the facts are too complex to be estimated with accuracy. Our Germanic ancestors accepted civilization when they met with it. Yes, but they met civilization under conditions peculiarly favorable to their own education. They had been more or less remotely influenced by its existence, centuries before they entered the field of history. When they entered this field, they met civilization first as formidable foes; they were long in contact with it without being themselves enslaved; and then later, in numerous cases, they met civilization as conquerors, who, in the course of their very efforts to conquer, found thus the

41

opportunity and later something of the leisure to learn, and who had time to discover by centuries of hard experience, how great were the advantages the cultivation of the Roman empire had to offer them. But suppose that Cæsar in the first century B.C. had already had the opportunity to undertake the civilization of Germany by means of our own modern devices. Suppose that he had then possessed unlimited supplies of rum, of rifles, and of machine guns. Suppose in brief that, by the aid of such gentle arts as we now often use, he had very greatly abbreviated the period of probation and of schooling that was open to the German barbarians to learn the lessons that the cultivated peoples had to teach. Suppose that Roman syndicates had been ready to take possession, at once, of the partly depopulated lands of the north, and to keep the few surviving natives thenceforth in their place, by showing them how cultivated races can look down upon savage folk. Well, in that case, the further history of civilization might have gone on without the aid of the Germanic peoples. The latter would then have quickly proved their natural inferiority once for all. They would have furnished one instance more for the race-partisans to cite in order to show how incapable the lower races are of ascending from barbarism to civilization. Dead men not only tell no tales; they also, strange to say, attend no schools, and learn no lessons. And hereby they prove themselves in the eyes of certain students of race-questions to have been always of a much lower mental type than the cultivated men who killed them. Their surviving descendants, if sufficiently provided with the means of corruption, and if sufficiently down-trodden, may remain henceforth models of degradation. For man, whatever his race, is an animal that you unquestionably can debase to whatever level you please, if you only have power, and if you then begin early enough, and devote yourself persistently enough to the noble and civilized task of proving him to be debased.

I do not doubt, then, that some races are more teachable than others. But I do very much doubt our power to estimate how teachable a race is, or what can be made of them, or what hereditary mental powers they have until we have given them centuries of opportunity to be taught. Fortune and the defects of the Roman Empire gave to the Germanic peoples an extraordinary opportunity to learn. So the world found out how teachable they were. Let their descendants not boast unduly until they, too, have given to other races, not indeed the opportunities of conquerors, but some equal opportunity to show of what sort of manhood they are capable.

Yet, you may insist, civilization itself had an origin. Were not the races that first won civilized rank superior in mental type to those that never showed themselves capable of such originality? Well, I reply, we do not know as yet precisely where, and still less how, civilization originated. But this seems clear, viz.: first, that physical environment and the forms of social aggregation which this environment determined, had a very great share in

making the beginnings of civilization possible; while, secondly, whatever part race-
qualities played in early civilization, certainly
no one race has the honor of beginning
the process. Neither Chinese nor Egyptian,
neither Caucasian nor Mongol, was the sole
originator of civilization. The African of the
tropical swamps and forests, the Australian
of the desert, the Indian of our prairies, was
sufficiently prevented by his physical environment from being the originator of a
great civilization. What each of these races
would have done in another environment,
we cannot tell. But the Indian of Central
America, of Mexico, and of Peru, shows us
that race alone did not predetermine how
remote from the origination of a higher civilization a stock must needs remain. Chinese
civilization, and, in recent times, Japanese
civilization, have shown us that one need not
be a Caucasian in order to originate a higher
type of wisdom.

In brief, then, there is hardly any one thing
that our actual knowledge of the human

mind enables us to assert, with any scientific exactness, regarding the permanent, the hereditary, the unchangeable mental characteristics which distinguish even the most widely sundered physical varieties of mankind. There is, to be sure, one exception to this rule, which is itself instructive. It is the case where we are dealing with physical and social degeneracy, the result of circumstances and of environment, and where such degeneracy has already gone so far that we have before us highly diseased human types, such as can no longer be reclaimed. But such types are not racial types. They are results of alcohol, of infection, or in some instances, of the long-continued pressure of physical environment. In such cases we can sometimes say, Here is a hopelessly degraded stock of men. But, then, civilization can create such stocks, out of any race of men, by means of a sufficient amount of oppression and of other causes of degradation, if continued through generations.

No race of men, then, can lay claim to a fixed and hereditary type of mental life such as we can now know with exactness to be unchangeable. We do not scientifically know what the true racial varieties of mental type really are. No doubt there are such varieties. The judgment day, or the science of the future, may demonstrate what they are. We are at present very ignorant regarding the whole matter.

VI

What, then, in the light of these considerations, is there which can be called fundamentally significant about our numerous modern race-problems? I answer, scientifically viewed, these problems of ours turn out to be not so much problems caused by anything which is essential to the existence or to the nature of the races of men themselves. Our so-called race-problems are merely the problems caused by our antipathies.

Now, the mental antipathies of men, like the fears of men, are every elemental, widespread, and momentous mental phenomena. But they are also in their fundamental nature extremely capricious, and extremely suggestible mental phenomena. Let an individual man alone, and he will feel antipathies for certain other human beings very much as any young child does — namely, quite capriciously — just as he will also feel all sorts of capricious likings for people. But train a man first to give names to his antipathies, and then to regard the antipathies thus named as sacred merely because they have a name, and then you get the phenomena of racial hatred, of religious hatred, of class hatred, and so on indefinitely. Such trained hatreds are peculiarly pathetic and peculiarly deceitful, because they combine in such a subtle way the elemental vehemence of the hatred that a child may feel for a stranger, or a cat for a dog, with the appearance of dignity and solemnity and even of duty which a name gives. Such antipathies will always play their part in human history. But what we can do about them is to try not to be fooled by them, not to take them too seriously because of their mere name. We can remember that they are childish phenomena in our lives, phenomena on a level with a dread of snakes, or of mice; phenomena that we share with the cats and with the dogs, not noble phenomena, but caprices of our complex nature.

Upon the theoretical aspects of the problem which such antipathies present, psychology can already throw some light. Man, as a social being, needs and possesses a vast range of simply elemental tendencies to be socially sensitive when in the presence of other men. These elemental tendencies appear, more or less untrained, in the bashfulness of childhood, in the stage fright of the unskilled, in the emotional disturbances of young people who are finding their way in the world, in the surprises of early love, in the various sorts of anthropophobia which beset nervous patients, in the antipathies of country folk toward strangers, in the excitements of mobs, in countless other cases of social stress or of social novelty. Such sensitiveness may arise in advance of or apart from any individual experience which gives a conscious reason why one should feel thus. A common feature of all such experiences is the fact that one human being finds other human beings to be *portentous*, even when the socially sensitive being does not in the least know why they should be so. That such reactions have an instinctive basis is unquestionable. Their general use is that they prepare one, through interest in men, to be ready for social training, and to be submissively plastic. In milder forms, or upon the basis of agreeable social relations, such instinctive emotions easily come to be moulded into the most fascinating of human interests; and the social life is impossible without this basis of the elemental concerns which man feels merely because of the fact that other men are there in his world. If decidedly intense, however, such instinctively determined experiences are apt, like other intense disturbances, to be prevailingly painful. And since novelty, oddity, and lack of social training on the part of the subject concerned are motives which tend to make such social reflexes intense, a very great number of the cruder and more childish social reactions involve antipathies; for a social antipathy is merely a painful, and so, in general, an overintense, reflex disturbance in the presence of another human being. No light need be thrown, by the mere occurrence of such an antipathy, upon any permanently important social character of the hated object. The chance intensity of the passing experience may be alone significant. And any chance association may serve to secure, in a given case, the intensity of disturbance which makes the object hated. Oddities of feature or of complexion, slight physical variations from the customary, a strange dress, a scar, a too steady look, a limp, a loud or deep voice, any of these peculiarities, in a stranger, may be, to one child, or nervous subject, or other sensitive observer, an object of fascinated curiosity; to another, slightly less stable observer, an intense irritation, an object of terror, or of violent antipathy. The significant fact is that we are all instinctively more or less sensitive to such features, simply because we are by heredity doomed to be interested in all facts which may prove to be socially important. Whether we are fascinated, or horror-stricken, or angry, is, apart from training, largely a matter of the momentary subjective intensity of the disturbance.

But all such elemental social experiences are *ipso facto*, highly suggestible. Our social training largely consists in the elimination or in the intensification or in the systematizing of these original reactions through the influence of suggestion and of habit. Hence the antipathy, once by chance aroused, but then named, imitated, insisted upon, becomes to its victims a sort of sacred revelation of truth, sacred merely because it is felt, a revelation merely because it has won a name and a social standing.

What such sacred revelations, however, really mean, is proved by the fact that the hungry traveller, if deprived of his breakfast long enough, by means of an accidental delay of his train, or the tired camper in the forest, may readily come to feel whatever racial antipathy you please toward his own brother, if the latter then wounds social susceptibilities which the abnormal situation has made momentarily hyperæsthetic.

I have said little or nothing, in this paper, of human justice. I have spoken mainly of human illusions. We all have illusions, and hug them. Let us not sanctify them by the name of science.

For my part, then, I am a member of the human race, and this is a race which is, as a whole, considerably lower than the angels, so that the whole of it very badly needs race-elevation. In this need of my race I personally and very deeply share. And it is in this spirit only that I am able to approach our problem.

II

PROVINCIALISM

II

I PROPOSE, in this address, to define certain issues which, as I think, the present state of the world's civilization, and of our own national life, make both prominent and critical.

I

The word "provincialism," which I have used as my title, has been chosen because it is the best single word that I have been able to find to suggest the group of social tendencies to which I want to call your especial attention. I intend to use this word in a somewhat elastic sense, which I may at once indicate. When we employ the word "provincialism" as a concrete term, speaking of "a provincialism," we mean, I suppose, any social disposition, or custom, or form of speech or of civilization, which is especially characteristic of a province. In this sense one speaks of the provincialisms of the local dialect of any English shire, or of any German country district. This use of the term in relation to the dialects of any language is very common. But one may also apply the term to name, not only the peculiarities of a local dialect, but the fashions, the manners, and customs of a given restricted region of any country. One also often employs the word "provincialism" as an abstract term, to name not only the customs or social tendencies themselves, but that fondness for them, that pride in them, which may make the inhabitants of a province indisposed to conform to the ways of those who come from without, and anxious to follow persistently their own local traditions. Thus the word "provincialism" applies both to the social habits of a given region, and to the mental interest which inspires and maintains these habits. But both uses of the term imply, of course, that one first knows what is to be meant by the word "province." This word, however, is one of an especially elastic usage. Sometimes, by a province, we mean a region as

restricted as a single English county, or as
the smallest of the old German principalities.
Sometimes, however, one speaks of the whole
of New England, or even of the Southern
states of our Union, as constituting one province; and I know of no easy way of defining
how large a province may be. For the term,
in this looser sense, stands for no deter-
minate political or legal division of a country.
Meanwhile we all, in our minds, oppose the
term " province " to the term " nation," as the
part is opposed to the whole. Yet we also often
oppose the terms "provincial" and "metropolitan," conceiving that the country districts and
the smaller towns and cities belong even to the
province, while the very great cities belong
rather to the whole country, or even to the
world in general. Yet here the distinction
that we make is not the same as the former
distinction between the part of a country and
the whole country. Nevertheless, the ground
for such an identification of the provincial
with that which pertains to country districts
and to smaller cities can only lie in the sup-

posed tendency of the great city to represent
better the interests of the larger whole than
do the lesser communities. This suppo-
sition, however, is certainly not altogether well
founded. In the sense of possessing local
interests and customs, and of being limited
to ideas of their own, many great cities are
almost as distinctly provincial as are certain
less populous regions. The plain people of
London or of Berlin have their local dialect;
and it seems fair to speak of the peculiarities
of such dialects as provincialisms. And
almost the same holds true of the other social
traditions peculiar to individual great cities.
It is possible to find, even amongst the highly
cultivated classes of ancient cities, ideas and
fashions of behavior as characteristically
local, as exclusive in their indifference to the
ways of outsiders, as are the similarly characteristic ways and opinions of the country
districts of the same nationality. And so
the opposition of the provincial to the metropolitan, in manners and in beliefs, seems to
me much less important than the other oppo-

sition of the province, as the more or less restricted part, to the nation as the whole. It is this latter opposition that I shall therefore emphasize in the present discussion. But I shall not attempt to define how large or how well organized, politically, a province must be. For my present purpose a county, a state, or even a large section of the country, such as New England, might constitute a province. For me, then, a province shall mean any one part of a national domain, which is, geographically and socially, sufficiently unified to have a true consciousness of its own unity, to feel a pride in its own ideals and customs, and to possess a sense of its distinction from other parts of the country. And by the term "provincialism" I shall mean, first, the tendency of such a province to possess its own customs and ideals; secondly, the totality of these customs and ideals themselves; and thirdly, the love and pride which leads the inhabitants of a province to cherish as their own these traditions, beliefs, and aspirations.

II

I have defined the term used as my title. But now, in what sense do I propose to make provincialism our topic? You will foresee that I intend to discuss the worth of provincialism, *i.e.* to consider, to some extent, whether it constitutes a good or an evil element in civilization. You will properly expect me, therefore, to compare provincialism with other social tendencies; such tendencies as patriotism, the larger love of humanity, and the ideals of higher cultivation. Precisely these will constitute, in fact, the special topics of my address. But all that I have to say will group itself about a single thesis, which I shall forthwith announce. My thesis is that, in the present state of the world's civilization, and of the life of our own country, the time has come to emphasize, with a new meaning and intensity, the positive value, the absolute necessity for our welfare, of a wholesome provincialism, as a saving power to which the world in the near future will need more and more to appeal.

62

PROVINCIALISM

The time was (and not very long since), when, in our own country, we had to contend against very grave evils due to false forms of provincialism. What has been called sectionalism long threatened our national unity. Our Civil War was fought to overcome the ills due to such influences. There was, therefore, a time when the virtue of true patriotism had to be founded upon a vigorous condemnation of certain powerful forms of provincialism. And our national education at that time depended both upon our learning common federal ideals, and upon our looking to foreign lands for the spiritual guidance of older civilizations. Furthermore, not only have these things been so in the past, but similar needs will, of course, be felt in the future. We shall always be required to take counsel of the other nations in company with whom we are at work upon the tasks of civilization. Nor have we outgrown our spiritual dependence upon older forms of civilization. In fact we shall never outgrow a certain inevitable degree of such dependence. Our national unity, moreover, will always require of us a devotion that will transcend in some directions the limits of all our provincial ideas. A common sympathy between the different sections of our country will, in future, need a constantly fresh cultivation. Against the evil forms of sectionalism we shall always have to contend. All this I well know, and these things I need not in your presence emphasize. But what I am to emphasize is this: The present state of civilization, both in the world at large, and with us, in America, is such as to define a new social mission which the province alone, but not the nation, is able to fulfil. False sectionalism, which disunites, will indeed always remain as great an evil as ever it was. But the modern world has reached a point where it needs, more than ever before, the vigorous development of a highly organized provincial life. Such a life, if wisely guided, will not mean disloyalty to the nation; and it need not mean narrowness of spirit, nor yet the further development of jealousies between various communities. What it will mean, or at least may mean, — this, so far as I have time, I wish to set forth in the following discussion. My main intention is to define the right form and the true office of provincialism, — to portray what, if you please, we may well call the Higher Provincialism, — to portray it, and then to defend it, to extol it, and to counsel you to further just such provincialism.

Since this is my purpose, let me at once say that I address myself, in the most explicit terms, to men and women who, as I hope and presuppose, are and wish to be, in the wholesome sense, provincial. Every one, as I maintain, ought, ideally speaking, to be provincial, — and that no matter how cultivated, or humanitarian, or universal in purpose or in experience he may be or may become. If in our own country, where often so many people are still comparative strangers to the communities in which they have come to live, there are some of us who, like myself, have changed our provinces dur-

65

ing our adult years, and who have so been unable to become and to remain in the sense of European countries provincial; and if, moreover, the life of our American provinces everywhere has still too brief a tradition, — all that is our misfortune, and not our advantage. As our country grows in social organization, there will be, in absolute measure, more and not less provincialism amongst our people. To be sure, as I hope, there will also be, in absolute measure, more and not less patriotism, closer and not looser national ties, less and not more mutual sectional misunderstanding. But the two tendencies, the tendency toward national unity and that toward local independence of spirit, must henceforth grow together. They cannot prosper apart. The national unity must not kill out, nor yet hinder, the provincial self-consciousness. The loyalty to the Republic must not lessen the love and the local pride of the individual community. The man of the future must love his province more than he does to-day. His provincial customs and ideals must be more and not less highly developed, more and not less self-conscious, well-established, and earnest. And therefore, I say, I appeal to you as to a company of people who are, and who mean to be, provincial as well as patriotic, — servants and lovers of your own community and of its ways, as well as citizens of the world. I hope and believe that you all intend to have your community live its own life, and not the life of any other community, nor yet the life of a mere abstraction called humanity in general. I hope that you are fully aware how provincialism, like monogamy, is an essential basis of true civilization. And it is with this presupposition that I undertake to suggest something toward a definition and defence of the higher provincialism and of its office in civilization.

III

With this programme in mind, let me first tell you what seem to me to be in our modern world, and, in particular, in our American world, the principal evils which are to be corrected by a further development of a true provincial spirit, and which cannot be corrected without such a development.

The first of these evils I have already mentioned. It is a defect incidental, partly to the newness of our own country, but partly also to those world-wide conditions of modern life which make travel, and even a change of home, both attractive and easy to dwellers in the most various parts of the globe. In nearly every one of our American communities, at least in the northern and in the western regions of our country, there is a rather large proportion of people who either have not grown up where they were born, or who have changed their dwelling-place in adult years. I can speak all the more freely regarding this class of our communities, because, in my own community, I myself, as a native of California, now resident in New England, belong to such a class. Such classes, even in modern New England, are too large. The stranger, the sojourner, the newcomer, is an inevitable factor in the life of most American communities. To make him welcome is one of the most gracious of the tasks in which our people have become expert. To give him his fair chance is the rule of our national life. But it is not on the whole well when the affairs of a community remain too largely under the influence of those who mainly feel either the wanderer's or the new resident's interest in the region where they are now dwelling. To offset the social tendencies due to such frequent changes of dwelling-place we need the further development and the intensification of the community spirit. The sooner the new resident learns to share this spirit, the better for him and for his community. A sound instinct, therefore, guides even our newer communities, in the more fortunate cases, to a rapid development of such a local sentiment as makes the stranger feel that he must in due measure conform if he would be permanently welcome, and must accept the local spirit if he is to enjoy the advantages of his community. As a Californian I have been interested to see both the evidences and the nature of this rapid evolution of the genuine provincial spirit in my own state. How swiftly, in that country, the Californians of the early days seized upon every suggestion that could give a sense of the unique importance of their new provincial life. The associations that soon clustered about the tales of the life of Spanish missionaries and Mexican colonists in the years before 1846, — these our American Californians cherished from the outset. This, to us often half-legendary past, gave us a history of our own. The wondrous events of the early mining life, — how earnestly the pioneers later loved to rehearse that story; and how proud every young Californian soon became of the fact that his father had had his part therein. Even the Californian's well-known and largely justified glorification of his climate was, in his own mind, part of the same expression of his tendency to idealize whatever tended to make his community, and all its affairs, seem unique, beloved, and deeply founded upon some significant natural basis. Such a foundation

was, indeed, actually there; nature had,
indeed, richly blessed his land; but the real
interest that made one emphasize and idealize
all these things, often so boastfully, was the
interest of the loyal citizen in finding his community an object of pride. Now you, who
know well your own local history, will be able
to observe the growth amongst you of this tendency to idealize your past, to glorify the
bounties that nature has showered upon you,
all in such wise as to give the present life of
your community more dignity, more honor,
more value in the eyes of yourselves and of
strangers. In fact, that we all do thus glorify
our various provinces, we well know; and
with what feelings we accompany the process,
we can all observe for ourselves. But it is
well to remember that the special office, the
principal use, the social justification, of such
mental tendencies in ourselves lies in the aid
that they give us in becoming loyal to our
community, and in assimilating to our own
social order the strangers that are within our
gates. It is the especial art of the colonizing

peoples, such as we are, and such as the English are, to be able by devices of this sort rapidly to build up in their own minds a provincial loyalty in a new environment. The French, who are not a colonizing people, seem to possess much less of this tendency. The Chinese seem to lack it almost altogether. Our own success as possessors of new lands depends upon this one skill in making the new lands where we came to dwell soon seem to us glorious and unique. I was much impressed, some years ago, during a visit to Australia and New Zealand, with the parallel developments in the Australasian colonies. They too have already their glorious past history, their unique fortunes, their romances of the heroic days, — and, in consequence, their provincial loyalty and their power to assimilate their newcomers. So learn to view your new community that every stranger who enters it shall at once feel the dignity of its past, and the unique privilege that is offered to him when he is permitted to belong to its company of citizens, — this is the first rule of the people of every colonizing nation when they found a new province.

Thus, then, I have pointed out the first evil with which our provincialism has to deal — the evil due to the presence of a considerable number of not yet assimilated newcomers in most of our communities. The newcomers themselves are often a boon and welcome indeed. But their failure to be assimilated constitutes, so long as it endures, a source of social danger, because the community needs well-knit organization. We meet this danger by the development of a strong provincial spirit amongst those who already constitute the centralized portion of the community. For thus a dignity is given to the social order which makes the newcomer long to share in its honors by deserving its confidence. But this aspect of provincialism, this usefulness of local pride, is indeed the best known aspect of my topic. I pass at once to the less frequently recognized uses of the provincial spirit, by mentioning the second of the evils with which a wise provincialism is destined to contend.

IV

This second modern evil arises from, and constitutes, one aspect of the levelling tendency of recent civilization. That such a levelling tendency exists, most of us recognize. That it is the office of the province to contend against some of the attendant evils of this tendency, we less often observe. By the levelling tendency in question I mean that aspect of modern civilization which is most obviously suggested by the fact that, because of the ease of communication amongst distant places, because of the spread of popular education, and because of the consolidation and of the centralization of industries and of social authorities, we tend all over the nation, and, in some degree, even throughout the civilized world, to read the same daily news, to share the same general ideas, to submit to the same overmastering social forces, to live in the same external fashions, to discourage individuality, and to approach a dead level of harassed mediocrity. One of the most

marked of all social tendencies is in any age
that toward the mutual assimilation of men
in so far as they are in social relations with one
another. One of the strongest human pre-
dispositions is that toward imitation. But
our modern conditions have greatly favored
the increase of the numbers of people who
read the same books and newspapers, who
repeat the same phrases, who follow the same
social fashions, and who thus, in general, imitate one another in constantly more and more
ways. The result is a tendency to crush the
individual. Furthermore there are modern
economic and industrial developments, too
well known to all of you to need any detailed
mention here, which lead toward similar
results. The independence of the small
trader or manufacturer becomes lost in the
great commercial or industrial combination.
The vast corporation succeeds and displaces
the individual. Ingenuity and initiative become subordinated to the discipline of an
impersonal social order. And each man,
becoming, like his fellow, the servant of mas-

ters too powerful for him to resist, and too complex in their undertakings for him to understand, is, in so far, disposed unobtrusively to conform to the ways of his innumerable fellow-servants, and to lose all sense of his unique moral destiny as an individual.

I speak here merely of tendencies. As you know, they are nowhere unopposed tendencies. Nor do I for an instant pretend to call even these levelling tendencies wholly, or principally, evil. But for the moment I call attention to what are obviously questionable, and in some degree are plainly evil, aspects of these modern tendencies. Imitation is a good thing. All civilization depends upon it. But there may be a limit to the number of people who ought to imitate precisely the same body of ideas and customs. For imitation is not man's whole business. There ought to be some room left for variety. Modern conditions have often increased too much what one might call the purely mechanical carrying-power of certain ruling social influences.

There are certain metropolitan newspapers, for instance, which have far too many readers for the good of the social order in which they circulate. These newspapers need not always be very mischievous ones. But when read by too vast multitudes, they tend to produce a certain monotonously uniform triviality of mind in a large proportion of our city and suburban population. It would be better if the same readers were divided into smaller sections, which read different newspapers, even if these papers were of no higher level. For then there would at least be a greater variety in the sorts of triviality which from day to day occupied their minds. And variety is the beginning of individual independence of insight and of conviction. As for the masses of people who are under the domination of the great corporations that employ them, I am here not in the least dwelling upon their economic difficulties. I am pointing out that the lack of initiative in their lives tends to make their spiritual range narrower. They are too little disposed to create their own world. Now every man who gets into a vital relation to God's truth becomes, in his own way, a creator. And if you deprive a man of all incentive to create, you in so far tend to cut him off from God's truth. Or, in more common language, independence of spirit flourishes only when a man at least believes that he has a chance to change his fortunes if he persistently wills to do so. But the servant of some modern forms of impersonal social organization tends to lose this belief that he has a chance. Hence he tends to lose independence of spirit.

Well, this is the second of the evils of the modern world which, as I have said, provincialism may tend to counteract. Local spirit, local pride, provincial independence, influence the individual man precisely because they appeal to his imitative tendencies. But thereby they act so as to render him more or less immune in presence of the more trivial of the influences that, coming from without his community, would otherwise be likely to reduce him to the dead level of the customs of the whole nation. A country district may seem to a stranger unduly crude in its ways; but it does not become wiser in case, under the influence of city newspapers and of summer boarders, it begins to follow city fashions merely for the sake of imitating. Other things being equal, it is better in proportion as it remains self-possessed, — proud of its own traditions, not unwilling indeed to learn, but also quite ready to teach the stranger its own wisdom. And in similar fashion provincial pride helps the individual man to keep his self-respect even when the vast forces that work toward industrial consolidation, and toward the effacement of individual initiative, are besetting his life at every turn. For a man is in large measure what his social consciousness makes him. Give him the local community that he loves and cherishes, that he is proud to honor and to serve, — make his ideal of that community lofty, — give him faith in the dignity of his province, — and you have given him a power to counteract the levelling tendencies of modern civilization.

V

The third of the evils with which a wise
provincialism must contend is closely connected with the second. I have spoken of
the constant tendency of modern life to the
mutual assimilation of various parts of the
social order. Now this assimilation may occur slowly and steadily, as in great measure
it normally does; or, on the other hand, it
may take more sudden and striking forms, at
moments when the popular mind is excited,
when great emotions affect the social order.
At such times of emotional disturbance, society is subject to tendencies which have
recently received a good deal of psychological
study. They are the tendencies to constitute
what has often been called the spirit of the
crowd or of the mob. Modern readers of
the well-known book of Le Bon's on "The
Crowd" well know what the tendencies to
which I refer may accomplish. It is true that
the results of Le Bon are by no means wholly
acceptable. It is true that the psychology of

large social masses is still insufficiently understood, and that a great many hasty statements have been made about the fatal tendency of great companies of people to go wrong. Yet in the complex world of social processes there can be no doubt that there exist such processes as the ones which Le Bon characterizes. The mob-spirit is a genuine psychological fact which occasionally becomes important in the life of all numerous communities. Moreover, the mob-spirit is no new thing. It has existed in some measure from the very beginning of social life. But there are certain modern conditions which tend to give the mob-spirit new form and power, and to lead to new social dangers that are consequent upon the presence of this spirit.

I use the term " mob-spirit " as an abbreviation for a very large range of phenomena, phenomena which may indeed be classed with all the rest of the imitative phenomena as belonging to one genus. But the mob-phenomena are distinguished from the other

imitative phenomena by certain characteristic emotional tendencies which belong to
excited crowds of people, and which do not
belong to the more strictly normal social
activities. Man, as an imitative animal, naturally tends, as we have seen, to do whatever his companions do, so long as he is not
somehow aroused to independence and to
individuality. Accordingly, he easily shares
the beliefs and temperaments of those who are
near enough to him to influence him. But
now suppose a condition of things such as may
readily occur in any large group of people
who have somehow come to feel strong sympathy with one another, and who are for any
reason in a relatively passive and impres-
sible state of mind. In such a company of
people let any idea which has a strong emotional coloring come to be suggested, by the
words of the leader, by the singing of a song,
by the beginning of any social activity that
does not involve clear thinking, that does not
call upon a man to assert his own independence.
Such an idea forthwith tends to take pos-

session in an extraordinarily strong degree of every member of the social group in question. As a consequence, the individual may come to be, as it were, hypnotized by his social group. He may reach a stage where he not merely lacks a disposition to individual initiative, but becomes for the time simply unable to assert himself, to think his own thoughts, or even to remember his ordinary habits and principles of conduct. His judgment for the time becomes one with that of the mass. He may not himself observe this fact. Like the hypnotized subject, the member of the excited mob may feel as if he were very independently expressing himself. He may say: "This idea is my own idea," when as a fact the ruling idea is suggested by the leaders of the mob, or even by the accident of the momentary situation. The individual may be led to acts of which he says: "These things are my duty, my sacred privilege, my right," when as a fact the acts in question are forced upon him by the suggestions of the social mass of which at the instant he is merely a helpless member. As the hypnotized subject, again, thinks his will free when an observer can see that he is obliged to follow the suggestions of the hypnotizer, so the member of the mob may feel all the sense of pure initiative, although as a fact he is in bondage to the will of another, to the motives of the moment.

All such phenomena are due to very deep-seated and common human tendencies. It is no individual reproach to any one of us that, under certain conditions, he would lose his individuality and become the temporary prey of the mob-spirit. Moreover, by the word "mob" itself, or by the equivalent word "crowd," I here mean no term that reflects upon the personal characters or upon the private intelligence of the individuals who chance to compose any given mob. In former ages when the defenders of aristocratic or of monarchical institutions used to speak with contempt of the mob, and oppose to the mob the enlightened portion of the community, the wise who ought to rule, or the

people whom birth and social position se-
cured against the defects of the mob, the term
was used without a true understanding of the
reason why crowds of people are upon occasion disposed to do things that are less intelligent than the acts of normal and thoughtful people would be. For the modern student
of the pyschology of crowds, a crowd or a mob
means not in any wise a company of wicked,
of debased, or even of ignorant persons.
The term means merely a company of people
who, by reason of their sympathies, have
for the time being resigned their individual
judgment. A mob might be a mob of saints
or of cutthroats, of peasants or of men of
science. If it were a mob it would lack due
social wisdom whatever its membership might
be. For the members of the mob are sympathizing rather than criticising. Their ruling
ideas then, therefore, are what Le Bon calls
atavistic ideas; ideas such as belong to earlier
and cruder periods of civilization. Opposed
to the mob in which the good sense of individuals is lost in a blur of emotion, and in

a helpless suggestibility, — opposed to the
mob, I say, is the small company of thoughtful individuals who are taking counsel together. Now our modern life, with its vast
unions of people, with its high development
of popular sentiments, with its passive and
sympathetic love for knowing and feeling
whatever other men know and feel, is subject to the disorders of larger crowds, of more
dangerous mobs, than have ever before been
brought into sympathetic union. One great
problem of our time, then, is how to carry on
popular government without being at the
mercy of the mob-spirit. It is easy to give
this mob-spirit noble names. Often you hear
of it as "grand popular enthusiasm." Often
it is highly praised as a loyal party spirit or
as patriotism. But psychologically it is the
mob-spirit whenever it is the spirit of a large
company of people who are no longer either
taking calm counsel together in small groups,
or obeying an already established law or custom, but who are merely sympathizing with
one another, listening to the words of leaders,

and believing the large print headings of their
newspapers. Every such company of people
is, in so far, a mob. Though they spoke with
the tongues of men and of angels, you could
not then trust them. Wisdom is not in them
nor in their mood. However highly trained
they may be as individuals, their mental
processes, as a mob, are degraded. Their
suffrages, as a mob, ought not to count.
Their deeds come of evil. The next mob
may undo their work. Accident may render their enthusiasm relatively harmless.
But, as a mere crowd, they cannot be wise.
They cannot be safe rulers. Who, then,
are the men who wisely think and rightly
guide? They are, I repeat, the men who
take counsel together in small groups, who respect one another's individuality, who meanwhile criticise one another constantly, and
earnestly, and who suspect whatever the
crowd teaches. In such men there need be
no lack of wise sympathy, but there is much
besides sympathy. There is individuality, and
there is a willingness to doubt both one

another and themselves. To such men, and to such groups, popular government ought to be intrusted.

Now these principles are responsible for the explanation of the well-known contrast between those social phenomena which illustrate the wisdom of the enlightened social order, and the phenomena which, on the contrary, often seem such as to make us despair for the moment of the permanent success of popular government. In the rightly constituted social group where every member feels his own responsibility for his part of the social enterprise which is in hand, the result of the interaction of individuals is that the social group may show itself wiser than any of its individuals. In the mere crowd, on the other hand, the social group may be, and generally is, more stupid than any of its individual members. Compare a really successful town meeting in a comparatively small community with the accidental and sometimes dangerous social phenomena of a street mob or of a great political convention. In the one case every individual may gain wisdom from his contact with the social group. In the other case every man concerned, if ever he comes again to himself, may feel ashamed of the absurdity of which the whole company was guilty. Social phenomena of the type that may result from the higher social group, the group in which individuality is respected, even while social loyalty is demanded, — these phenomena may lead to permanent social results which as tradition gives them a fixed character may gradually lead to the formation of permanent institutions, in which a wisdom much higher than that of any individual man may get embodied. A classic instance of social phenomena of this type, and of the results of such social activities as constantly make use of individual skill, we find in language. However human language originated, it is certain that it was never the product of the mob-spirit. Language has been formed through the efforts of individuals to communicate with other individuals. Human speech is, therefore, in its structure, in its devices, in its thoughtfulness, essentially the product of the social activities of comparatively small groups of persons whose ingenuity was constantly aroused by the desire of making some form of social coöperation definite, and some form of communication amongst individuals effective. The consequence is that the language of an uncultivated people, who have as yet no grammarians to guide them and no literature to transmit the express wisdom of individual guides from generation to generation, may, nevertheless, be on the whole much more intelligent than is any individual that speaks the language.

Other classic instances of social processes wherein the group appears wiser than the individual are furnished to us by the processes that resulted through centuries of development in the production of the system of Roman law or of the British constitution. Such institutions embody more wisdom than any individual who has taken part in the production of these institutions has ever possessed. Now the common characteristic of all such social products seems to me to be due to the fact that the social groups in which they originated were always such as encouraged and as in fact necessitated an emphasis upon the contrasts between various individuals. In such groups what Tarde has called "the universal opposition" has always been an effective motive. The group has depended upon the variety and not the uniformity of its members. On the other hand, the other sort of social group, the mob, has depended upon the emotional agreement, the sympathy, of its members. It has been powerful only in so far as they forgot who they individually were, and gave themselves up to the suggestions of the moment.

It follows that if we are to look for the source of the greatest dangers of popular government, we must expect to find them in the influence of the mob-spirit. Le Bon is right when he says that the problem of the future will become more and more the problem how to escape from the domination of the crowd. Now I do not share Le Bon's pessimism when he holds, as he seems to do, that all popular government necessarily involves the tendency to the prevalence of the mob-spirit. So far as I can see Le Bon and most of the other writers who in recent times have laid so much stress upon the dangers of the mob, have ignored, or at least have greatly neglected, that other social tendency, that tendency to the formation of smaller social groups, which makes use of the contrasts of individuals, and which leads to a collective wisdom greater than any individual wisdom. But why I do insist upon this is that the problem of the future for popular government must involve the higher development, the better organization, the more potent influence, of the social groups of the wiser type, and the neutralization through their influence of the power of the mob-spirit. Now the modern forms of the mob-spirit have become so portentous because of a tendency that is in itself very good, even as may be the results to which it often leads. This tendency is that toward

a very wide and inclusive human sympathy,
a sympathy which may be as undiscriminat-
ing as it often is kindly. Sympathy, however, as one must recollect, is not necessarily
even a kindly tendency. For one may sympathize with any emotion, — for instance,
with the emotions of a cruelly ferocious mob.
Sympathy itself is a sort of neutral basis
for more rational mental development. The
noblest structures may be reared upon its
soil. The basest absurdities may, upon occasion, seem to be justified, because an undis-
criminating sympathy makes them plausible.
Now modern conditions have certainly tended,
as I have said, to the spread of sympathy.
Consider modern literature with its disposition to portray any form of human life, however ignoble or worthless, or on the other
hand, however lofty or inspiring, — to portray it not because of its intrinsic worth but
because of the mere fact that it exists. All
sorts and conditions of men, — yes, all sorts
and conditions of emotion, however irrational,
have their hearing in the world of art to-day,

win their expression, charm their audience, get, as we say, their recognition. Never were men so busy as now with the mere eagerness to sympathize with, to feel whatever is the lot of any portion of humanity. Now, as I have said, this spread of human sympathy, furthered as it is by all the means at the disposal of modern science, so far as that science deals with humanity, is a good thing just in so far as it is a basis upon which a rational philanthropy and a more intelligent social organization can be founded. But this habit of sympathy disposes us more and more to the influence of the mob. When the time of popular excitement comes, it finds us expert in sharing the emotions of the crowd, but often enervated by too frequent indulgence in just such emotion. The result is that modern mobs are much vaster, and in some respects more excitable than ever they were before. The psychological conditions of the mob no longer need include the physical presence of a crowd of people in a given place. It is enough if the newspapers, if the theatre,

if the other means of social communication,
serve to transmit the waves of emotional enthusiasm. A nation composed of many mill-
ions of people may fall rapidly under the
hypnotic influence of a few leaders, of a few
fatal phrases. And thus, as our third evil,
we have not only the general levelling tendency of modern social life, but the particular
tendency to emotional excitability which tends
to make the social order, under certain conditions, not only monotonous and unideal,
but actively dangerous.

Yet, as we have seen, this evil is not, as Le
Bon and the pessimists would have it, inherent
in the very fact of the existence of a social
order. There are social groups that are not
subject to the mob-spirit. And now if you
ask how such social groups are nowadays to
be fostered, to be trained, to be kept alive for
the service of the nation, I answer that the
place for fostering such groups is the province,
for such groups flourish under conditions that
arouse local pride, the loyalty to one's own
community, the willingness to remember one's

own ways and ideals, even at the moment
when the nation is carried away by some
levelling emotion. The lesson would then be:
Keep the province awake, that the nation may
be saved from the disastrous hypnotic slumber
so characteristic of excited masses of mankind.

IV

I have now reviewed three types of evils
against which I think it is the office of provincialism to contend. As I review these
evils, I am reminded somewhat of the famous
words of Schiller in his "Greeting to the New
Century," which he composed at the outset
of the nineteenth century. In his age, which
in some respects was so analogous to our own,
despite certain vast differences, Schiller found
himself overwhelmed as he contemplated the
social problem of the moment by the vast
national conflict, and the overwhelming forces
which seemed to him to be crushing the more
ideal life of his nation, and of humanity.
With a poetic despair that we need indeed no
longer share, Schiller counsels his reader, in

certain famous lines, to flee from the stress of
life into the still recesses of the heart, for, as he
says, beauty lives only in song, and freedom
has departed into the realm of dreams. Now
Schiller spoke in the romantic period. We
no longer intend to flee from our social ills
to any realm of dreams. And as to the recesses of the heart, we now remember that
out of the heart are the issues of life. But so
much my own thesis and my own counsel
would share in common with Schiller's words.
I should say to-day that our national unities
have grown so vast, our forces of social consolidation have become so paramount, the resulting problems, conflicts, evils, have been so
intensified, that we, too, must flee in the pursuit of the ideal to a new realm. Only this
realm is, to my mind, so long as we are speaking of social problems, a realm of real life. It
is the realm of the province. There must
we flee from the stress of the now too vast and
problematic life of the nation as a whole.
There we must flee, I mean, not in the sense
of a cowardly and permanent retirement, but

in the sense of a search for renewed strength, for a social inspiration, for the salvation of the individual from the overwhelming forces of consolidation. Freedom, I should say, dwells now in the small social group, and has its securest home in the provincial life. The nation by itself, apart from the influence of the province, is in danger of becoming an incomprehensible monster, in whose presence the individual loses his right, his self-consciousness, and his dignity. The province must save the individual.

But, you may ask, in what way do I conceive that the wise provincialism of which I speak ought to undertake and carry on its task? How is it to meet the evils of which I have been speaking? In what way is its influence to be exerted against them? And how can the province cultivate its self-consciousness without tending to fall back again into the ancient narrowness from which small communities were so long struggling to escape? How can we keep broad humanity and yet cultivate provincialism? How can we be loyally patriotic, and yet preserve our consciousness of the peculiar and unique dignity of our own community? In what form are our wholesome provincial activities to be carried on?

I answer, of course, in general terms, that the problem of the wholesome provincial consciousness is closely allied to the problem of any individual form of activity. An individual tends to become narrow when he is what we call self-centred. But, on the other hand, philanthropy that is not founded upon a personal loyalty of the individual to his own family and to his own personal duties is notoriously a worthless abstraction. We love the world better when we cherish our own friends the more faithfully. We do not grow in grace by forgetting individual duties in behalf of remote social enterprises. Precisely so, the province will not serve the nation best by forgetting itself, but by loyally emphasizing its own duty to the nation and therefore its right to attain and to cultivate its own unique wisdom. Now all this is indeed obvious enough, but this is precisely what in our days of vast social consolidation we are some of us tending to forget.

Now as to the more concrete means whereby the wholesome provincialism is to be cultivated and encouraged, let me appeal directly to the loyal member of any provincial community, be it the community of a small town, or of a great city, or of a country district. Let me point out what kind of work is needed in order to cultivate that wise provincialism which, as you see, I wish to have grow not in opposition to the interests of the nation, but for the very sake of saving the nation from the modern evil tendencies of which I have spoken.

First, then, I should say a wholesome provincialism is founded upon the thought that while local pride is indeed a praiseworthy accompaniment of every form of social activity, our province, like our own individuality, ought to be to all of us rather an ideal than a mere boast. And here, as I think, is a matter which is too often forgotten. Everything valuable is, in our present human life, known to us as an ideal before it becomes an attainment, and in view of our human imperfections, remains to the end of our short lives much more a hope and an inspiration than it becomes a present achievement. Just because the true issues of human life are brought to a finish not in time but in eternity, it is necessary that in our temporal existence what is most worthy should appear to us as an ideal, as an Ought, rather than as something that is already in our hands. The old saying about the bird in the hand being worth two in the bush does not rightly apply to the ideal goods of a moral agent working under human limitations. For him the very value of life includes the fact that its goal as something infinite can never at any one instant be attained. In this fact the moral agent glories, for it means that he has something to do. Hence the ideal in the bush, so to speak, is always worth infinitely more to him than the food or the plaything of time that happens to be just now in his hands. The differ-

ence between vanity and self-respect depends
largely upon this emphasizing of ideals in the
case of the higher forms of self-consciousness,
as opposed to the emphasis upon transient
temporal attainments in the case of the lower
forms. Now what holds true of individual
self-consciousness ought to hold true of the
self-consciousness of the community. Boast-
ing is often indeed harmless and may prove a
stimulus to good work. It is therefore to be
indulged as a tribute to our human weakness.
But the better aspect of our provincial consciousness is always its longing for the improve-
ment of the community.

And now, in the second place, a wise provincialism remembers that it is one thing to
seek to make ideal values in some unique
sense our own, and it is quite another thing
to believe that if they are our own, other
people cannot possess such ideal values in
their own equally unique fashion. A realm
of genuinely spiritual individuality is one
where each individual has his own unique
significance, so that none could take another's

place. But for just that very reason all the unique individuals of the truly spiritual order stand in relation to the same universal light, to the same divine whole in relation to which they win their individuality. Hence all the individuals of the true spiritual order have ideal goods in common, as the very means whereby they can win each his individual place with reference to the possession and the employment of these common goods. Well, it is with provinces as with individuals. The way to win independence is by learning freely from abroad, but by then insisting upon our own interpretation of the common good. A generation ago the Japanese seemed to most European observers to be entering upon a career of total self-surrender. They seemed to be adopting without stint European customs and ideals. They seemed to be abandoning their own national independence of spirit. They appeared to be purely imitative in their main purposes. They asked other nations where the skill of modern sciences lay, and how the new powers were to be gained by them. They seemed to accept with the utmost docility every lesson, and to abandon with unexampled submissiveness, their purpose to remain themselves. Yet those of us who have watched them since, or who have become acquainted with representative Japanese students, know how utterly superficial and illusory that old impression of ours was regarding the dependence, or the extreme imitativeness, or the helpless docility, of the modern Japanese. He has now taught us quite another lesson. With a curious and on the whole not unjust spiritual wiliness, he has learned indeed our lesson, but he has given it his own interpretation. You always feel in intercourse with a Japanese how unconquerable the spirit of his nation is, how inaccessible the recesses of his spirit have remained after all these years of free intercourse with Europeans. In your presence the Japanese always remains the courteous and respectful learner so long as he has reason to think that you have anything to teach him. But he remains as absolutely his own master with regard to the interpretation, the use, the possession of all spiritual gifts, as if he were the master and you the learner. He accepts the gifts, but their place in his national and individual life is his own. And we now begin to see that the feature of the Japanese nationality as a member of the civilized company of nations is to be something quite unique and independent. Well, let the Japanese give us a lesson in the spirit of true provincialism. Provincialism does not mean a lack of plasticity, an unteachable spirit; it means a determination to use the spiritual gifts that come to us from abroad in our own way and with reference to the ideals of our own social order.

And therefore, thirdly, I say in developing your provincial spirit, be quite willing to encourage your young men to have relations with other communities. But on the other hand, encourage them also to make use of what they thus acquire for the furtherance of the life of their own community. Let them win aid from abroad, but let them also

have, so far as possible, an opportunity to use
this which they acquire in the service of their
home. Of course economic conditions rather
than deliberate choice commonly determine
how far the youth of a province are able to
remain for their lifetime in a place where they
grow up. But so far as a provincial spirit is
concerned, it is well to avoid each of two extremes in the treatment of the young men of
the community, — extremes that I have too
often seen exemplified. The one extreme
consists in maintaining that if young men
mean to be loyal to their own province, to
their own state, to their own home, they ought
to show their loyalty by an unwillingness to
seek guidance from foreign literature, from
foreign lands, in the patronizing of foreign
or distant institutions, or in the acceptance of
the customs and ideas of other communities
than their own. Against this extreme let the
Japanese be our typical instance. They have
wandered far. They have studied abroad.
They have assimilated the lore of other communities. And they have only gained in

local consciousness, in independence of spirit, by the ordeal. The other extreme is the one expressed in that tendency to wander and to encourage wandering, which has led so many of our communities to drive away the best and most active of their young men. We want more of the determination to find, if possible, a place for our youth in their own communities.

Finally, let the province more and more seek its own adornment. Here I speak of a matter that in all our American communities has been until recently far too much neglected. Local pride ought above all to centre, so far as its material objects are concerned, about the determination to give the surroundings of the community nobility, dignity, beauty. We Americans spend far too much of our early strength and time in our newer communities upon injuring our landscapes, and far too little upon endeavoring to beautify our towns and cities. We have begun to change all that, and while I have no right to speak as an æsthetic judge concerning the growth of the love of the beautiful in our country, I can strongly insist that no community can think any creation of genuine beauty and dignity in its public buildings or in the surroundings of its towns and cities too good a thing for its own deserts. For we deserve what in such realms we can learn how to create or to enjoy, or to make sacrifices for. And no provincialism will become dangerously narrow so long as it is constantly accompanied by a willingness to sacrifice much in order to put in the form of great institutions, of noble architecture, and of beautiful surroundings an expression of the worth that the community attaches to its own ideals.

III

ON CERTAIN LIMITATIONS OF THE THOUGHT-FUL PUBLIC IN AMERICA

III

ON CERTAIN LIMITATIONS OF THE THOUGHT-FUL PUBLIC IN AMERICA [1]

NO one who is engaged in any part of the work of the higher education in this country can doubt that, at the present time, our thoughtful public, — the great company of those who read, reflect, and aspire, — is a larger factor in our national life than ever before. When foreigners accuse us of extraordinary love for gain, and of practical materialism, they fail to see how largely we are a nation of idealists. Yet that we are such a nation is something constantly brought to the attention of those whose calling requires them to observe any of the tendencies prevalent in our recent intellectual life in America.

I

When I speak, in this way, of contemporary American idealists, I do not now specially refer

[1] An address first delivered at Vassar College.

to the holders of any philosophical opinions, or even to the representatives of any one type of religious faith. I here use the term in no technical sense. In this discussion, I mean by the word "idealist," a man or woman who is consciously and predominantly guided, in the purposes and in the great choices of life, by large ideals, such as admit of no merely material embodiment, and such as contemplate no merely private and personal satisfaction as their goal. In this untechnical sense the Puritans were idealists. The signers of our Declaration of Independence were idealists. Idealism inspired us during our Civil War. Idealism has expressed itself in the rich differentiation of our national religious life. Idealism has founded our colleges and universities.

Well, using the term "idealism" in this confessedly untechnical sense, I say that many of our foreign judges have failed to see how largely we Americans are to-day a nation of idealists. To be sure, we are by no means alone amongst modern men in our idealism.

But elsewhere sometimes the consequences of long-continued and oppressive militarism, sometimes the stress of certain social problems, and sometimes the burdens of ancient imperial responsibility, have tended more to discourage, or even quite to subdue, many forms of that fidelity to ideals upon which surely all higher cvilization in any country depends. But, with us, ever since the close of the Civil War, numerous forces have been at work to render us as a nation more thoughtful, more aspiring, and more in love with the immaterial things of the spirit, and that too even at the very moment when our material prosperity, with all of its well-known corrupting temptations, has given us much opportunity, had we chosen to take it, to be what the mistaken foreign critics often suppose us to be, — a people really sunk in practical materialism.

Moreover, in saying all this, as to our general growth in spiritual interests, I am not at all unmindful of that other side, — that grosser material side of our national life, upon which our foreign critics so often insist.

The growth of unwise luxury, the brute power of ill-used wealth, the unideal aspects of our political life, the evils of our great cities, — what enlightened American is there who does not recognize the magnitude of such ills in our midst? But you cannot prove the absence of light merely by exploring the darker chasms and caverns of our national existence. Vast as are those recesses of night, the light of large and inspiring ideas shines upon still vaster regions of our American life. Side by side with the excesses of mere luxury you find, amongst our people, a true and increasing, a self-sacrificing and intelligent love of the beautiful for its own sake. Side by side with the misuse of money, you observe the encouraging frequency of the great and humane deeds that wealth can do. Nor is this all. An ardent and often successful struggle for social reform, and a civic pride that aims, sometimes even from the very depths of municipal degradation, at the accomplishment of great and honorable public services, — these are tendencies that are growing amongst us, and that are never wholly or permanently checked even by the closest contact with the very worst of our national defects.

Yet, of course, the real proof of the prevalence of what I have called idealism, in the great masses of our people, is above all to be sought not in any particular good deeds of wealthy men, nor yet in the public life of the great cities, but in the intellectual and religious life of the community at large. And here it is, as I say, that the college teacher, or any other worker professionally concerned with the higher mental interests of our people, has a chance to estimate the strength and magnitude of these interests in the unseen.

In our country it is extraordinarily easy, and as one may at once admit it is too easy, to get a hearing for any seemingly new and large-minded doctrine relating either to social reform or to inspiring changes of creed. Whoever desires the reputation of the founder of a new sect has merely to insist upon his plan for reforming society and saving souls, —

has merely to announce repeatedly to the public the high valuation that he sets upon his own ideas concerning nobler topics in order to win a respectful hearing from many, and, if his ideas have any measure of coherence and of humanitarian interest, an often all too kindly acquiescence from at least a few. And the faithfulness of these few may soon assume the pathetic intensity that so often marks the devotion of the followers of small sects. Need I mention many instances in order to remind you of the nature of these now so familiar processes in our American life? The late Mr. Henry George was, up to the time of the appearance of his "Progress and Poverty," a man quite unknown to the nation at large, — a California newspaper man, with no obvious authority to teach concerning economic problems. His book received, at the time of its appearance, little or no support from the professional economists, and excited at first, I believe, little very close attention from their side. George himself was no party manager. He used hardly any showy devices for attracting popular attention. He was simply in earnest. Yet we all know how the sect of his followers grew. And any busy man who has sometimes received letters from propagandists of that particular sect will also know, I suppose, how humane, how faithful, how strenuous, how unworldly, and one may add, how unweariedly obstinate they may be in their efforts to convert the doubter and to lead people to see, and if possible to love, their new way of social salvation. A similar, and even more swiftly contagious kindliness made possible the dramatic, if temporary, success of Mr. Bellamy's book, " Looking Backward." And again, a case in point is the movement in connection with which Bryan gained his first national prominence in 1896, a movement which came near proving successful, and which was then for a time so dangerous. That movement had its origin quite as much in practical idealism as in material distress. Its fundamental motives were in considerable measure philanthropic, humane, and, in an abstract way, vaguely large-minded. That was precisely what made this movement most dangerous. Unwise philanthropy, uninstructed large-mindedness, can often prove injurious to the very interests they seek to further. Our greatest national danger now lies in an extravagant love of ideally fascinating enterprises, whose practical results are as hard to foresee and to estimate as was the end that lay before the noble-hearted Childe Rolande of Browning's well-known poem, when he searched for the goal of his journey in the midst of the shifting landscapes, and the treacherous pathways of his romantic wilderness.

Well, these, I say, are instances of our American idealism in social matters. In religion, a similar tendency has been strong in our life from the very first. It has not only multiplied sects among us, but it has also wrought great good by giving lasting strength to their missionary and to their other philanthropic enterprises. Moreover it has endowed them with an importance for the daily life of the people that no established State church could ever have won by a merely external show of authority. The same interest in ideals has kept the sects themselves from stagnation, has insisted upon an adjustment of whatever in their fashions of teaching was non-essential to the vital needs of each generation of people. On the other hand, this idealism often shows itself less worthily in the form of a hasty desire for whatever seems new, or remote, or fantastic in faith. At the present day there is hardly a conceivable creed about ultimate matters, be it never so quaint or so unreasonable that, if its apparent intents are only humane, and its catch words impressive, this creed once earnestly taught cannot very quickly find a body of adherents, not only in our country at large, but in some of the most thoughtful and sophisticated communities which our country contains. It is not the ignorant amongst us who are the prey of strange new doctrines, so much as a portion of the most considerate classes of our public. And we are indeed not obliged to be bigoted in order to feel that, at present, this spiritual plasticity of our American public has gone too far. We ought to be docile; but the disposition to prove all things can easily outrun the power to hold fast that which is good.

As a consequence, if new sects thus easily find followers, and often faithful and permanent followers, there is also the other side of the picture. There are those of our people who waste life in merely floating from doctrine to doctrine. In such minds the art of holding fast has wholly been lost, in favor of the easier art of at least playing with all the things that belong in the realms of the spirit. For such souls, new doctrines are like new pictures, or new plays, or like the passing events of a social season. The more ardent amongst such people grow temporarily enthusiastic upon every new occasion where they listen to what they cannot comprehend. The more disillusioned find the novelties in doctrine more or less of a bore, just as some folk always find the plays and the parties tedious. But both the ardent and the disillusioned, in such social groups as I now have in mind, do indeed treat the new doctrines and the various rival plans of salvation altogether too much as they treat the social occasions, the plays, or the pictures. They expect something new to take the place of the old at each moment of their experience. And whether ardent or bored they continue their life-long quest for spiritual sensations.

Such excesses of the higher life in our country are only too easy to observe and, upon occasion, to ridicule. I have not mentioned them however for the sake, of ridicule. Spinoza said that human affairs are neither to be wept over nor to be laughed at, but to be understood; and Spinoza's word, despite its seeming fatalism, had from any point of view its large measure of truth. I am speaking at present of symptoms. These symptoms, like other incidents of so complex a life as ours, have both their good and their evil aspects. Devotion to ideals has its dangers as it has its glories. I have to point out the one as an aid toward a comprehension of the other.

I turn to still other and better aspects of the tendency here in question. If one asks what the devotion to ideals has of late accomplished with purest success in the intellectual life of our country, I myself should be disposed to name, as one of the noblest, most positive, and most unsullied products of American idealism in recent years, the whole modern educational movement. The reform of academic methods and interests, both in the younger and in the older universities and colleges has been such, within the past twenty-five years, as to constitute one of the most substantial and significant events in our national history. The general public still understands all too little of the vast work that has been accomplished. By the fault of too large a portion of the newspaper press of the country the more trivial aspects of our academic life, — the public athletic contests, and the idle gossip of the hour, — are continually exaggerated, while the serious and the most progressive tendencies of this same life are as persistently slighted and are often misrepresented. Yet despite the false perspective in which our colleges are thus often made to appear, the general public has nevertheless somehow learned to support nobly the interests of academic reform. The vast sums that have been dedicated to the cause of learning, the cordial approval that our more enlightened people have given to the attempts at bettering higher education, — these have been most encouraging features of our educational movement. Nor has this movement confined itself to the Universities and Colleges. In its connection with the lower schools it is still in the period of storm and stress and hope. But it is indeed, in all its forms, a movement in the interest of ideals. It has needed at every step great sacrifices, strenuous devotion, wide sympathies, and far-reaching foresight. And these have been forthcoming. When an intelligent American wants to vindicate the honor of his country to foreigners, I know in our recent history of no purer instance of single-hearted patriotism, devoted to humane and unsullied ideals, and successful against all sorts of foes, not only without but within,— I know, I say, of no purer instance of such true patriotism than is furnished by just the great educational reform movement, and especially the academic movement of the last quarter of a century. For this has indeed been no mere effort of dreamers. It has been a practical movement. It has been guided by administrators who were often of the highest executive talent, — men quite capable, in many instances, of winning worldly success in wholly different and more showy regions of public life. It has been supported by benefactors who were often tempted by all sorts of more selfish interests to use their wealth otherwise. It has given to great numbers of youth a light and guidance that have meant for them escape from spiritual bondage, and an opportunity to become in their turn benefactors. It has furnished to our country a constantly increasing class of cultivated workers, ready to enter practical life with the ardor of a genuine idealism in their hearts and minds. And great as this academic movement has been, its influence is only beginning. Its real fruits are still to be gathered.

So far, then, I have surveyed a number of forms of recent American idealism. I have meant to be fair to both sides of the shield. Not all golden is our devotion to ideals. Yet this devotion is too marked a feature of our national spirit to justify the neglect of those among our foreign critics who regard us as mainly workers for wealth, or as lovers of mere material power. It may not be unfitting, upon this occasion, for us to ask ourselves what can yet be done to make our national idealism more intelligent, better organized, and, above all, more effective.

II

For, after all that we have thus far said, when we try to sum up the amount of influence exerted by these various forms of idealism upon the actual life of our country, we are obliged to confess that our thoughtful public is not yet as efficacious as it ought to be. Too frequently we find the lovers of the ideal engaged in unprofitable conflicts with their spiritual kindred. Plan wars with plan; reform stands in hostile array over against reform. Meanwhile the children of this world are wiser in their generation than the children of light. The people who dwell in the realms of thought and of higher faith consequently find themselves unable to organize effectively their reforms. They indeed associate, discourse, and take counsel together. But their enemies remain too often the better managers. While, as I just said, the academic movement is the great instance amongst us, in recent times, of the possible practical success of ideal interests, this educational progress stands too much alone. Our tree of life flourishes, and puts forth countless leaves; but it does not yet bear sufficient fruit for the healing of the nation. Our national idealism is more characteristic of our intellectual and religious life than it is productive of permanent, organized, and substantial results. Whenever the servants of ill perfect their devices for corrupting anywhere the state, and misusing its resources, the lovers of good things find themselves too frequently helpless to thwart such mischief. Yet amongst us the conscious servants of ill are really in a very decided minority. Our youth are exceptionally high-minded and aspiring. Our social life is full of admirable purposes. Our people are very generally interested in the things of the spirit. Yet the enemy seems to have possession of far too many of the effective weapons of social and of political warfare. When we try to meet him in the field, we are too scattered, too fantastic, or too uncertain in mind, to be ready for an effective fight. Our thoughtfulness involves too much idle curiosity, too much vaguely restless ardor, too much unwillingness to accept the necessary material limitations under which human work is to be done. And therefore we are indeed often, in practical undertakings, "beaten down" like Tennyson's

Lancelot in his quest for the Grail, "beaten down by little men, mean knights." The enemy, the power of evil at work, in whatever form in our land, — the enemy at least always knows his own purpose. But we, we lovers of the ideal, spend far too much of our time vaguely wandering from one club-meeting or lecture or recent book to another, trying to discover just what it is that we are thinking about. While we, with eager minds, inquire into the shifting thing sometimes called the New Thought, the enemy is steadily engaged in serving the purposes of the Old Adam. And those purposes need no course of lectures to define them, no laborious clambering toward any "higher plane" to survey them. The devil within is always ready to explain them directly and personally to all comers. The consequence is precisely that appearance of grosser materialism which our foreign critics falsely take to be characteristic of our country. But much more characteristic of us is the intensity, the manifoldness, the restlessness, and in all but a few regions,

128

the relative ineffectiveness of our national idealism.

Look where you will, even in the regions where ideas best and most beneficently express themselves in our social life, and you find the same limitations of our thoughtful public exemplified, setting bounds to our spiritual progress even in the best regions of our activity, and resulting in too many cases, in a more or less complete inability to do wholesome reforming work where work is most needed. In speaking thus, I have in mind no one section of our country, no one type of activity, no one special class of our thoughtful public. As myself a Californian, and as one often called upon to visit, in connection with professional duties, very various parts of our land, I have felt the limitations of which I speak in the West as well as in the East, amongst good men and women, in the life of the professional classes as well as in the life of the people of the world.

Wherever you go, you find the typical American sensitive to ideas, curious about doctrines, concerned for his soul's salvation, still more concerned for the higher welfare of his children, willing to hear about great topics, dissatisfied with merely material objects, seeking even wealth rather with a view to its more ideal uses than with a mere desire for its sensuous gratifications, disposed to plan great things for his country and for his community, proud of both, jealous of their honor, and discontented with the life that now is. His piety has its ideal fervor none the less when it is the piety of the free thinker than when it is that of the faithful. He forms and supports great associations for public-spirited ends. He encourages science and learning. He pauses in the midst of the rush of business to discuss religion, or education, or psychical research, or mental healing, or socialism. His well-known and characteristic devotion to his children keeps fresh in his heart a childlike love of plans and hopes and beliefs that belong not so much to the market-place, as to the far-off future, and to the home land of the Platonic ideas.

Yet this same American is unable to give his idealism any adequate expression in his social life. His country towns and his manufacturing cities are too often full of hideous ugliness. Even the best of his great cities are in appearance whatever they happen to be. In founding new cities and in occupying new lands he first devotes himself to burning the forests, to levelling with ruthless eagerness the hill-slopes, to inflicting upon the land, whatever its topography, the unvarying plan of his system of straight streets and of rectangular street crossings. In brief, he begins his new settlements by a feverish endeavor to ruin the landscape. Now all this he does not at all because he is a mere materialist but (as a colleague of mine, Professor George Palmer, has pointed out), he does this because mere nature is, as such, vaguely unsatisfactory to his soul, because what is merely found must never content us, and because our present life itself is felt to be not yet ideal. Hence, the first desire is to change, to disturb, to bring the new with us.

In the regions thus so quickly altered by man's hand, a community spirit, a strong local pride, quickly springs up. The church, the school, the university, appear within a very few years, and seem at first as if they were quite at home. One is firmly determined, in each young community, that they shall all be the best of their kind anywhere to be found. The social order thus established has also its representative literature, — its poets, its artists, its public heroes, even its swiftly acquired local traditions, as well as its self-conscious social independence, somewhat too ardently and tremulously asserted, of the mere worn-out ideals and authority of the older regions of the country.

Nor are the interests in ideal things confined to such expressions. Confident faith in the future and in the might of the new life asserts itself in such newer regions of our land in the overhasty construction of great railways, that pierce the mountains or invade the deserts, long before a less restlessly ideal people would have seen sufficient prospect of any adequate return for the material outlay. Our pioneer makers of railways have often seemed as if they were themselves amongst the prophets, the poets, or even the fanatics of our newer communities. But the result of this eagerness is too often a swift bankruptcy. The young community flies too near the sun, and then lies prostrate and wingless in the despair of hard times.

Hereupon begins the grosser period. The community soon really possesses through mere accumulation more wealth and power; yet merciless money-getters have profited by the failures of the first period, and these now take possession of the creations of the pioneers, crush out weaker opponents, obtain too much influence in local politics, and give to the life of the community just that outward seeming of mere materialism of which we have spoken. And now the better men learn more thoughtfully to look about them, only to observe, at this stage, what vast opportunities have been lost, what noble natural beauties have been hopelessly defaced, what ideal kingdoms have been carelessly created only to be conquered by the enemy.

The real struggle with evil herewith begins. The social order, so hastily and easily organized at the outset, through the finely ideal political instincts of our people, now becomes infected by various political diseases. Corruption grows too prominent in politics. The Philistines seem to have captured and blinded the Sampson whose deeds made the pioneer days so wonderful. Satan seems to have triumphed.

Yet this triumph is never so real as it seems. The good are still in the majority. The heart of society is still healthy. The church, the school, the university, the public library, the literary circles, the intellectual clubs, — these not only remain, but multiply, and in these one finds centres for the propagation of ideal interests. Would-be reformers become numerous. But alas, they war among themselves. They are too often crude, strident, prejudiced. Greed too often wins possession of the strongest material forces of the community. The reformers lift their too familiar voices in vain. The prophets true and false speak their many words. Many listen and applaud. Yet at the elections the prophets do not win. The thoughtful public remains the most characteristic, but too often the least effective, portion of the community.

Such is the tale of too many of our newer communities. Shall I speak still of the older communities? There indeed the processes are more complex; but the lesson, like the outcome, is too often the same. The great limitation of our thoughtful public in America remains its inability to take sufficient control of affairs. And in pointing out this limitation, I have already indicated, in a measure, both its causes and the directions in which we ought to look for a cure, if a cure is possible, for this ineffectiveness of our American idealism. Let me pass then to a closer study of this latter aspect of the case. I have not undertaken this discussion for the sake of merely criticising my brethren; but for the sake of suggesting some few ways of improving our state, in so far as any poor suggestions of mine can hope to possess value.

III

Yet, as I go on to this side of our topic, I must indeed admit quite freely that I have no panacea, no quack remedy to suggest, as any infallible cure for the ineffectiveness of our national idealism, or as any one saving device for overcoming the limitations of our thoughtful public. Such ills as the one here in question always lie deep in the very constitution of our temperaments. We cannot, by merely taking thought, add a cubit to our stature. One of the very limitations of our thoughtful public which are here under discussion lies in the fact that many of us suppose great reforms to be possible merely through good resolutions. Yet good resolutions have their place in accomplishing reforms. Our mere human consciousness never by itself transforms our temperaments; but it may do something toward lessening their ill effects, and toward intensifying or enlarging the range of their good qualities. Where limitations have to be overcome, a due measure of consciousness as to where the fault lies does not come amiss. Accordingly, with a full sense of the little that I can do by such mere practical advice as lies within my scope, I still wish not merely to point out the ailment, but to show how it may be attacked. That it is no hopeless ailment, such successes of our idealism as the modern educational movement have already shown us. May we not hope to escape in time and at last, in a measure from the ineffectiveness that now besets the efforts of the thoughtful people of our country?

Reform, in such matters, must come, if at all, from within. The kingdom of heaven is within you; and that truth is precisely what all ideally minded people know. It is this knowledge which makes them lovers of the unseen. I cannot then offer any pedagogical device for raising the thoughtful public of our country to a higher level of effectiveness, unless my device appeals directly to the individual.

137

The public as a whole is whatever the processes that occur, for good or for evil, in individual minds, may determine. No one of us is individually called upon for any very large share in determining other peoples' lives. The work of any one man, in this life, has a narrow range. Yet, on the other hand, the forest is made of the trees; and great reforms are due to the combined action of numerous individuals.

I appeal then to the individual lover of ideals. I say, upon such as you are, and upon such as you aspire to be, the future of our country depends. If you fail, in union with your spiritual kind, to win, and to win for good, the controlling voice in the nation's affairs, corruption, grossness, despotism, social ruin, will sooner or later make naught of our liberties, of all the dear memory of our country's fathers, and of the great work that we in America ought to do for mankind. And if such as you are find not the way to overcome, in time, these present limitations of the effectiveness of our thoughtful public, you will fail to win and to retain control of the constantly increasing complications of our national life. Our ideals will grow vaguer and more rest-less, even while our material activities become more steadily enchained by the powers of evil. We shall end where others have ended, in national disaster, in social dissolution, in humiliation, in the clutches of some domestic or foreign conqueror.

But in case you win effective control over your personal ideals and over your own pro-cesses of giving them expression, you your-self as an individual will indeed accomplish but an infinitesimal portion of the nation's vast task. Yet still it will be the nation's task in which, in your measure, you will be engaged. For no man liveth unto himself, and no man dieth unto himself. I appeal then to you, and to the public, only through such as you are. If you, together with the others who love the coming of the kingdom of heaven, succeed in solving your personal problems, the good cause will win in public as in private. And what you need to find is

139

some little task that you can effectually do. That task you need to perform.

To the individual, then, I address myself. Nor do I forget that I am speaking to students who already know what one means by high ideals, and by hearty aspirations, and who stand at the beginning of life's great tasks. There comes a sad time in many lives, when people who have long struggled in vain with foes without and foes within, grow weary of the cultivation of ideal interests. Those to whom I am especially privileged to speak, upon this occasion, have not reached this stage. I hope that when any of you reach it, you will pass it successfully, for nothing better have we in this life than our ideals and our hopes, and our power to do a little work. Just now you are privileged to have a faith, still unsullied, in such ideals, and a hope to do good work. I want to indicate some of the ways in which one may wisely nourish this faith, and undertake this work.

IV

My first word of advice, addressed thus especially to the thoughtful amongst us, relates to a certain moderation, to a certain temperance, that, as I believe, we must all cultivate in dealing with our own consciousness of what our ideals are. Devotion to what we believe to be a high cause demands of us, indeed, a certain thoroughness of surrender, a certain persistence in service, which, in its own due time and place, ought to know indeed no bounds. On the other hand, when thoughtful people cultivate ideals, they do so, in part, by thinking over these ideals, by reasoning about them, by becoming conscious of what they are, by trying to convert others to these ideals, and, in general, by giving these ideals articulate expression. The faithfulness of the unlearned may be dumb, half-conscious, incapable of giving any reason for itself. The fidelity of the thoughtful seeks definite formulation in a creed, propagates its cause by spoken and by written words, voices itself in

141

a doctrine that can be defended or assailed by argument, — in brief, seeks to add knowledge to faith, insight to service, and teaching to example. You often hear how important it is to be not only devoted, but wise, clear of head as well as persistent in service. Now such tendencies are an important factor in the lives of all thoughtful people. Their highest expression is a reasoned philosophy, which undertakes to investigate, to compare, to harmonize, and then, finally, to formulate and to teach systems of ideals. Now I am myself by calling a teacher of philosophy. I believe in persistent thoughtfulness as a most important factor in the higher life of humanity. I try to become as conscious as I properly can become of what my ideals are, and of why I hold them, and of how they go together to make one whole, and of why other lovers of reason ought, if I am right, to accept my ideals. Over against the inconsiderate partisans of this or of that form of unreasoning faith, I often have, as teacher of philosophy, to maintain the importance, for certain great purposes, of giving a reason for the faith that is in us. And so, as you see, I am in every way disposed to favor, in its place, not only the thoughtful spirit of inquiry, but the disposition to formulate ideals in a definite and conscious way, to maintain them through argument, and to propagate them by the spoken and by the written word. I believe in the human reason, as a vastly important factor in the development of all our ideals.

And yet, — I can here speak all the more frankly just because my profession is that of the reasoner, — I constantly see mischief done by an unwise exaggeration of the tendency to reason, to argue, to trust to mere formulas, to seek for the all-solving word; in brief, to bring to consciousness what for a given individual ought to remain unconscious. Thoughtfulness is, for us in this life, like any other human power and privilege. It must be exercised with a proper moderation. Thought must indeed be free. But freedom means responsibility. Thought, in any individual, must freely set limits to its own finite task. And when the thoughtful lovers of ideals forget this fact, they may become mere wranglers, or doctrinaires, or pedants, or, on the other hand, in the end, through failure in thinking, they may become cynics. Now some may wonder that, as a teacher of philosophy, I should at once lay the first stress upon this defect of the lovers of ideals, as a defect so often attendant upon the processes of unhappy thinkers. Some may wonder that I first confess the errors of my own calling. Yet why should I not do so? What defects has one more occasion to observe than those which occur in the erring human effort to pursue his own calling? If one loves his calling and believes in it, does he therefore ignore these defects? Shall one make a business of the art of seeing clearly, and yet entirely ignore the imperfections that may naturally beset his own organ of vision?

Very well then, I first observe that many thoughtful lovers of ideals, many students, many reformers, many teachers, are too much disposed to trust to constant argument, reasoning, or reflection, to keep them faithful to their own ideals, and to win others to these ideals. Or again, some lovers of the ideal, even when they profess not to argue, but to be followers of intuition, still in many cases are too fond of abstract formulas, of catch words or phrases. Such mistake fads for eternal truths. Now all such have not observed the inevitable limitations of the human thinking process in each individual mind. They do not observe that any one of us can think clearly and reflectively and can formulate exactly and successfully only in case we think with due moderation, and think during the time properly set apart for thought, trying to formulate only what we have more or less expert right to understand, and then devoting the rest of life to näiveté and to relatively unreflective action. As a professional reasoner, I have a profound contempt for deliberate excesses in the work of reasoning; I personally try to avoid such excesses. As one busy with formulating theories, I have a great hatred for the excessive use of formulas.

I remember well, from my student days, a pathetic incident that may illustrate the spirit in which I make this confession. While I was studying philosophy, one winter at Leipzig, I enjoyed many happy hours in company with a musical friend of mine, an advanced student at the Conservatory, who had devoted himself since childhood to the violin, and who has since won an important place in his profession. He often took me to attend the musical evenings at the Conservatory, and so helped me, as a mere listener, to enter the wondrous world of tones where he was making his home. But alas! for the moment, my friend, although so faithful and advanced a student of music, was himself no public performer at the Conservatory evenings, although in previous years he had been a prominent and favorite student player. Overwork had given him, for the time, one of those well-known functional nervous troubles of coördination, or "occupation disorders";

namely, in his case, a "violinist's arm." Neuralgic pains whenever he played had forced him to suspend his efforts. Prolonged rest for his arm was needed. My friend was perforce spending this year in the study of musical theory, and in other more general intellectual tasks relating to his art. Naturally this forced restraint was hard, and wounded ambition would often express itself; but still my friend was a man of general mental skill, who had therefore not a few resources in his distress. One evening we were together at the Conservatory. Many students played. Among them my friend's principal contemporary and rival, a young violinist of no small skill, won abounding applause by a very brilliant performance. And my friend, sitting beside me with wounded wing, must merely listen! It would have been more than human not to rebel a little. But my friend could at least remember that he himself had his own variety of mental occupations. He did remember this fact, yet he grieved inwardly and deeply. As we were walking home he was silent for a time, and then his wrath at the chains that bound him burst forth. We spoke of the rival. We could not avoid the topic. "Confound that fellow!" said my friend. "Confound that fellow; he can't do anything *but* fiddle!"

Well, I speak somewhat in my friend's general spirit, although I hope without any bitterness toward any particular rival student when I now say: "I am indeed not nearly as much of a reasoner as I desire to be. My skill in this art is far below my ambition. But, poor as I am, reasoning is indeed my own art. I love it. I prize it. I cultivate it. It is a great part of my life. And yet, — and yet I still insist, — let that reasoner, that thoughtful lover of ideals, that philosopher, if such there be, let him be confounded who cannot do anything *but* reason." And in the same way I say to you of the thoughtful public: Woe unto the man or woman who can do nothing but be thoughtful.

Yet why do I thus warn you? Pedantry, it will be said, is a disease of professors and of bookish men. The young, the ardent, and the general company of the faithful to ideals in our land, whatever their faults, are surely not pedants. An overcultivation of the merely abstract reason is not a besetting sin of most people. I reply that there are many forms of pedantry; there are many grounds for being on one's guard against it. The misuse of the reasoning process enters the life of the thoughtful in more ways than one. The love of abstract formulas, of mere phrases, or of falsely simplified thoughtful processes is not confined to the professors.

I remember once discussing with a young lady who was a college student of psychology, some points in the text-book of my honored colleague Professor William James. We spoke in particular of his wonderful chapter on Habit, so full, as some of you may know, not only of theoretical wisdom, but of wholesome practical advice about the formation and control of habits. I asked my young friend what she thought of this chapter. She

149

replied, with adorable näiveté, that she had found this chapter full of advice which must be very valuable indeed "for the young men for whom it was intended." Well, my young friend had certainly observed part of the significance of Professor James's chapter; but she did not admit having observed that his comments upon Habit apply to us all, whether young men or not. And now, just so, I should be sorry to have my word about the misuse of reason and the false love of abstract formulas supposed to apply only to those philosophers, if such there be, for whom it was indeed also intended. The lesson is general, and human. Especially does it apply to all the thoughtful public of America.

For this fault of a too abstract thoughtfulness is committed, in substance, whenever people try to reform all the world, or even any great region of our complex lives, by insisting upon any one set of phrases, of human conceptions and words, which the individual himself has found somehow dear to his own consciousness. Not merely the partisans of

technical reasoning, but the apostles of intuition, too, can commit our fault, whenever they
trust in any mere abstraction. The people
of one idea, the people to whom this or that
single device for saving souls is alone important,
the followers of fads, — these fall prey to this
form of error. They mistake the power to
define for the power to accomplish, the abstraction for the life, the single thought for
all the wealth of truth that our human world
contains, the exercise of an individual reason
for the whole task of reforming our nature.
And does not our modern America, both in the
East and in the West, really suffer too much,
nowadays, from mere fads? What shall
I do to be saved? says the inquirer, — and
the answer is, — "Practise this or that
system of mind cure, whose teaching can be
made clear in just so many lessons. Follow
Delsarte, study your attitudes, or oratory, or
some other formal accomplishment. Accept
this or that doctrine of the New Thought."
Now the people who cultivate ideals in this
spirit often suppose themselves to be free

from the philosopher's overwrought love of the reason. "We follow," they say, "spiritual intuitions. We thus avoid abstractions and wrangling." "Yes," one may reply, "but you none the less are anxious for some all-embracing formula, some one saving principle that shall do all manner of work." Now the human mind, in its present form of consciousness, is simply incapable of formulating all its practical devices under any one simple rule. We have to learn both to work and to wait. We have to learn to obey as well as to formulate. What saves the world can never be any one man's formulated scheme. Restless search for the immediate presence of the ideal is often vain, like the pioneer idealism that burns the forests merely to see what they hide. Let the forests grow. They are better than the empty hillsides. Much of the best in human nature simply escapes our present definitions, is known only by its fruits, and prospers best in the forest shade of unconsciousness. But a thoughtful lover of ideals, whether a philosopher or not, is of course thinking of something that he *can* formulate, — is trying to make his ideas conscious, explicit, teachable, and so abstract. Hence so much of his life's business as he best formulates is likely for that very reason to be narrow when compared with his whole human task and with his own best and deepest aims. We are primarily creatures of instinct; and instinct is not merely the part of us that allies us with the lower animals. The highest in us is also based upon instinct. And only a portion of your instincts can ever be formulated. You will be able in this life to tell what they mean in only a few instances. But your life's best work will depend upon all of your good instincts together. Hence a great part of your life's work will never become a matter of your own personal and private consciousness at all. It is one of the duties then of the thoughtful lover of ideals to know that he cannot turn into conscious thinking processes all of his ideal activities. Accordingly, he must indeed cultivate a wise näiveté, and that alongside of his reflective processes. That is why the companionship of children becomes the more useful to us the more thoughtful we are. They show us the beauty of unconsciousness, and help us to compensate for our tendency to abstraction by reminding us of what it is to live straightforwardly.

And now, I say, this rule of mine applies to the very lover of ideals whom I now chance to be addressing. We who teach philosophy are constantly receiving inquiries from people who seem not to know how little in human life can as yet be reduced to any abstractly stateable formulas at all. Teachers inquire as to the final and correct theory of the development of the human mind, as to the precise number of powers that the mind possesses, or as to the one secret of method in education. Newspapers or magazines call for popular discussions of the most serious and complex issues, as if these could finally be dealt with in any brief shape. A newspaper once asked me to contribute to a so-called symposium whose problem was to be this: What character-

istics will the ideal man of the future possess?
As I only knew about the ideal future man
this, that when he comes, he will, as in him
lies, adequately attend to his own business,
I felt unable to contribute anything original
to the proposed discussion. The first condition of knowing how to think about ideal
subjects consists in being aware not only what
can be profitably formulated at all, but when
and for what purpose a given formulation
is profitable. When I visit a convalescent
friend who is beginning to feel joyous after a
long illness, I do not in general discuss the
problem of evil. When I too am to enjoy the
company of my friend, I do not first undertake
to inquire into the metaphysical problem as to
whether my friend exists at all. And yet just
such problems have their place in philosophy.
Now just so, when I vote, since, as it chances,
I am no expert in sociology or in economic
problems, I generally have no really very
good reason that I can formulate, in a conscious
and philosophical way, why I vote just as I do.
I vote largely on grounds of sympathy and of

instinct. I know better than to try to do otherwise. If I tried to formulate a political theory, it would be a very poor one; for I have no scientific comprehension of politics, no philosophy adequate to directing my choice of parties. For my business is largely with other branches of philosophy. I am a member of one or two deliberative bodies, where I often hear lengthy debates upon complex practical questions. The debates for a time instruct me; but later they often weary me, if they continue, without instructing me. When people ask me my reason for my own vote in such complex practical cases, or wonder why I am anxious for a vote to be reached, I often say that just because my profession is reasoning, I have learned to know some of the limits of the art, and to recognize that about some complex practical issues, after a certain point, it is vain to reason further, since only personal reactions, incapable of adequate reflective formulation, will decide. Hence I grow weary of the much speaking. I know that at such times I seem unreasonable; but I merely want to vote; and more formulations will in such cases make me no wiser.

People often say that men act upon conscious reasoning processes, and women upon intuitions which they refuse to formulate. The assertion is, like most proverbial assertions, inadequate to the wealth of life's facts. Certainly women often enough act with a mysterious swiftness of unconscious wisdom. But so do many of the most effective men. I have, however, often observed that some educated women, some women who enter public life as reformers, and perhaps too many college-bred women, are nowadays troubled with an overfondness both for mere formulas and for abstract arguments about complex practical issues that only a happy instinctive choice and wholesome sentiment can ever successfully decide so long as we remain what we are; namely, frail and ignorant human beings, who see through a glass darkly. The fault of being overfond of abstractions, or of trying to formulate bad reasons for one's instinctive actions, does not characterize the man of business or the successful executive. One does not meet this fault in the market-place. But just this fault does characterize some of our most cultivated and thoughtful people in this country. And among these people I find a good many intellectual women.

What then is the happy medium? Shall I cease to think? No, not so. Be thoughtful, reason out some of your ideals for yourself. Know something, and know that something well. Have the region where you have a right to mistrust your instincts, to be keenly and mercilessly critical, to question, to doubt, and to formulate, and then devotedly to maintain and to teach. But let that region be the little clearing in your life's forest, — the place where you see, and comprehend, and are at home. Let there be such a place. You need it. It may be art, or theology, or Greek, or administrative work, or politics, or philosophy, or domestic economy, or general business, wherein you find this your chosen intellectual dwelling. In that region be indeed the crea-

ture of hard-won insight, of clear consciousness, of definite thinking about what it is
yours to know. There the formula is in order.
There the ideal is won by your investigations,
and defended by your arguments. I say,
have such a region. We need those who know.
In that region, believe only when you know
why you believe. But remember, life is vast,
and your little clearing is very small. In the
rest of life, cultivate näiveté, accept authority,
dread fads, follow as faithfully as your instinct permits other lovers of the ideal who are
here wiser than you, and be sure that though
your head splits you will never think out all
your problems, or formulate all your ideals
so long as you are in this life. If this precept
were followed in this country there would be
more experts, and fewer popular crazes,
more effective work done, and less time wasted
in hopeless efforts at general reforms. *De
te fabula*, I say to every studious soul who is
disposed to be too thoughtful rather than
wisely effective. Be in your devotion to effective leaders relatively uncritical in many things,

in order to be thoughtfully knowing in some. Be childlike in much of life in order to become maturely wise in some things.

V

If you are once aware of the vanity of trying to formulate everything, and to argue about all sorts of problems, you will not be tempted to pursue unwisely mere novelties of formulation for their own sake. I have spoken more than once of the feverish desire for new ideas in which our thoughtful public wastes much time. An entirely false interpretation of the doctrine of evolution has led some people to imagine that in any department of our lives, novelty as such must mean true progress toward the goal. Hence you constantly hear of the New Education, the New Psychology, the New Thought, the New Humanity, and whatever else can be adorned by the mere prefixing of this adjective. And yet people do not speak adoringly of the New Blizzard, or of the

New Weather in general. We all of us have a fondness, not altogether wise, for the so-called news of the day, quite apart from its meaning; and the newspapers daily verify for us the ancient fact that bad men lie and steal and murder. Such news, which alas is no news, but the ancient sorrow of our race, we do indeed greet with a certain keenness of interest which is neither altogether rational nor highly ideal. But still the lovers of the ideal do not in such cases suppose that some new form of burglary must, because of the fatal law of evolution, be higher in nature, or nobler, or more worthy of study than the older arts of the thieves. So nobody preaches in praise of the New Burglary. Nor do we suppose that evolution implies, as any universal law, that the New Blizzard, when it comes, is an object worthy of admiration above all former caprices of our climate. We know that if news, in this sense, is indeed interesting, still the weather is the weather, and the thieves break through and steal, and that no news makes more ideal these ancient aspects of the visible world. Now much that is proposed as new in thought, or in the less exact sciences, or in complex arts such as education, has indeed its importance as embodying real progress. When we know that to be the case, we welcome the new, not because it is merely new, but because it is a substantial addition to what is already known to be a good. But, on the other hand, much that is novel in opinion is novel only as the latest change of the weather is new. And I warn you, not indeed blindly to condemn, but cautiously to suspect doctrines that are obliged to advertise, very ostentatiously, the supposed fact that they are new, in order to get a public hearing. In really progressive sciences, as for instance in psychology itself, the most important advances need not be thus loudly heralded. They make their own way, not because they are merely new, but because they are maturely conceived and carefully worked out. As for the world of faith, it is as vain to be a mere seeker of novelties as it is to be a mere conservative. In our deeper faiths the newest

162

and the oldest of humanity's deeds, interests, and experiences lie side by side. What is new for one soul is not new for another. Love and death and our duty, these are the oldest and the newest things in human destiny. The new love is not on that account the true one. The new coming of death teaches still the ancient lessons of the burial psalm. The new duty is no duty unless it is an example of the most venerable of truths. "These things" says Antigone, "are not of to-day or of yesterday, and no man knows whence they came." As a fact, what you and I really most need and desire is not the new, nor yet the old. It is the eternal. The genuine lover of truth is neither a conservative nor a radical. He is beyond that essentially trivial opposition. He cares nothing for the time in which these things came to pass. For him their interest lies in their truth. Time is but an image, an imitation of the eternal. Evolution itself is only a fashion in which the everlasting appears. For God there is nothing new. Before the mountains were brought forth, or ever thou hadst founded the earth, from everlasting thou art God.

Be docile then; be ready to learn what is new to you. But avoid this disease of merely running after every thought that loudly proclaims, or every plan that stridently asserts, "Behold, I am new." Say to every such claimant for your reverence: "Are you such that you can grow old and still remain as good as ever? Then indeed I will trust you."

But is there nothing, then, in the idea of progress? Are there not certainly progressive movements, whose new stages will therefore be good? Yes. The actual discoveries of empirical science, once submitted to careful test, do indeed form a progressive series. Here the new, once assured by critical verification, is good. But the existence in any particular field of inquiry or of action of a progress that you and I can regard as certain, is never something to be merely presumed. The presumption is valid only after due examination. Only the expert can decide then, with clearness, whether the new is good.

164

This holds in finance and in business as genuinely as in politics or in religion. Therefore it is only, once more, within the relatively narrow range of your expertness, that you can judge whether the new really is, as such, likely to be the good. Outside of that range, favor no novelties unless they appeal to your personal sentiments, to your most humane sympathies, to your best cultivated, but still in general partly unconscious, tastes and instincts. In brief, then, I say to our thoughtful public, overcome your limitations, first by minute and faithful study of a few things and by clearness of ideas about them; then by childlike simplicity in the rest of life, by faithfulness to enlightened leaders, by resignation as opposed to restlessness, and above all by work rather than by idle curiosity. Organize through a willingness to recognize that we must often differ in insight, but that what we need is to *do* something together. Avoid this restless longing for mere novelty. Learn to wait, to believe in more than you see, and to love not what is old or new, but what is eternal.

IV

THE PACIFIC COAST

A PSYCHOLOGICAL STUDY OF THE RELATIONS OF CLIMATE AND CIVILIZATION

IV

THE PACIFIC COAST

A PSYCHOLOGICAL STUDY OF THE RELATIONS OF
CLIMATE [1] AND CIVILIZATION

I HAVE been asked to describe some of the principal physical aspects of California, and to indicate the way in which they have been related to the life and civilization of the region. The task is at once, in its main outlines, comparatively simple, and in its most interesting details hopelessly complex. The topography of the Pacific slope, now well known to most travellers, is in certain of its principal features extremely easy to characterize. The broad landscapes, revealing very frequently at a glance the structure of wide regions, give one an impression that the meaning of the whole can easily be comprehended. Closer study shows how difficult it is to understand the relation of precisely such features to the life that has grown up in this region.

[1] An address prepared for the National Geographical Society, in 1898.

The principal interest of the task lies in the fact that it is our American character and civilization which have been already moulded in new ways by these novel aspects of the far western regions. But we stand at the beginning of a process which must continue for long ages. Any one interested in the unity of our national life, and in the guiding of our destinies by broad ideals, desires to conceive in some fashion how the physical features of the Pacific Coast may be expected to mould our national type. Yet thus far we have, as it were, only the most general indications of what the result must be.

In endeavoring to distinguish between what has already resulted from physical conditions and what has been due to personal character, to deliberate choice, or to the general national temperament, or to what we may have to call pure accident, one is dealing with a task for which the data are not yet sufficient. We can but make a beginning.

THE PACIFIC COAST

I

The journey westward to California is even now, when one goes by rail, a dramatic series of incidents. From the wide plains of the states immediately west of the Mississippi one passes at first through richly fertile regions to the more and more arid prairies of the eastern slope of the Rocky Mountains. Then come either the steep ranges or the wide passes, and at last what used to be called the Great American Desert itself, that great interior basin of the rugged, saw-tooth ranges, where the weirdly dreary landscape at once terrifies the observer by its desolation, and inspires him by the grandeur of its loneliness, and by the mysterious peacefulness of the desert wherein, as one at first feels, nothing like the complex and restless life of our eastern civilization will ever be possible.

As one travels by the familiar central route still further west, one reaches the valley of the Humboldt River, that kindly stream whose general westerly trend made the early overland migration possible. At the end of

this portion of the route rises the vast wall of
the Sierra Range, and the traveller's heart
thrills with something of the strange feeling
that the early immigrants described when,
after their long toil, they reached the place
where, just beyond this dark and deathlike
wall, the land of heavenly promise was known
to lie. Abrupt is the ascent of this great
range; slower on the other side, the descent,
amidst the magnificent cañons of the western
slope, to the plains of the Sacramento Valley.
From the foot-hills of the Sierra one used to
the journey could easily get at many points a
wide outlook into the region beyond. The
Coast Range in the far distance bounds with
its blue summits the western view, and seems
to hide the ocean for whose shore one already
looks, as in childhood I, who then lived in the
Sierra foot-hills, and had never seen the sea,
used longingly to look. Through the valley
beneath winds the Sacramento, fed by numerous tributaries from the Sierra. At length, as
one continues the railway journey, one reaches
the plains of the Sacramento Valley them-

selves, and enters that interesting region where the scattered oaks, separated from one another by wide distances, used to seem, I remember in the old days, as if set out by God's hand at the creation in a sort of natural park. One crosses the valley, — the shore of San Francisco Bay is reached. If one is travelling in summer, the intensely dry heat of the Sacramento Valley suddenly gives place to the cold winds of the coast. Mist and the salt air of the sea greet you as you approach the rugged hills about the Golden Gate, and find your way by ferry to San Francisco.

The region that to-day is so swiftly and so easily entered was of old the goal of an over-land tour that might easily last six months from the Missouri River, and that was attended with many often-recorded dangers. Yet the route that in this brief introductory statement we have followed, is nearly identical with the one which first guided the immigrants to the new land. And in part this route was identical, namely, as far as Fort Hall, with the once familiar Oregon Trail.

II

Oregon and California, the Canaan which long formed the only goal of those who travelled over these intermediate regions, are determined as to their characters and climate by the presence beyond them of the great ocean, and by the trend northward and southward of the elevated ranges of mountains which lie west of the central basin. On all the continents of the world, in the latitudes of the temperate zones, the countries that lie on the lee side of the ocean receive the world's prevailing winds tempered by a long course over the water. Accordingly, those countries very generally enjoy a relatively steadier climate than those which lie in the same latitudes but on the lee side of the great continental areas; that is, toward the east. But other influences join themselves, as secondary causes, in a number of cases, to this general consequence of the prevailing west winds of the temperate zones. The good fortune of Oregon and California as to their climate

174

depends, in fact, as the meteorologists now recognize, partly upon the steadying influence of the vast masses of water that there lie to windward, partly upon the influence of the mountain masses themselves in affecting precipitation, and finally upon certain great seasonal changes in the distribution of the more permanent areas of high and low pressure, — changes which have been elaborately studied in the report of Lieutenant Glassford on the climate of California and Nevada, published as a government document in 1891.

During the summer months, the entire region west of the high Sierra Range and of its continuation, the Cascade Range, is comparatively free, and in the southern portion almost wholly free, from storm disturbances. The moisture-laden winds of the ocean are then deflected by areas of high pressure, which persist off the coast, and the moister winds are prevented from coming into close relation to the mountains and discharging their moisture. On the other hand, during the months from November to March, and in Oregon still later, storm areas are more frequent, and their behavior along the coast, by reason of certain areas of high pressure which are then established in the regions east of the Sierra, is rendered different from the behavior more characteristic of the well-known storms of our eastern coast. The resulting conditions are sometimes those of long-continued and decidedly steady precipitation on the Coast Range of California, and on the western slope of the Sierra, as well as throughout the Oregon region. Thus arise the longer rains of the California wet season. At other times in the rainy season the storm areas, moving back and forth in a more variable way along the coast, but still unable to pass the area of high pressure that lies farther inland, produce conditions of a more gently and variably showery sort over a wide extent of country; as the rainy season passes away in March and April, these showers grow less frequent in California, though they continue in Oregon much later. That portion of Oregon which lies east of the Cascade Range belongs,

176

once more, to the decidedly dry regions of the
western country; on the other hand, western
Oregon has a much moister climate than
California.

In consequence, the climate, throughout
this entire far western region, is characterized by a very sharp distinction between the
wet and dry seasons; while otherwise, within
the area of Oregon and California, there exist
very wide differences as to the total amount
of annual precipitation. Wide extents of
country, as, for instance, the San Joaquin Valley in California, have needed the development of elaborate methods of irrigation. The
relative variability of rainfall in the more
northern regions has in some years beset the
Sacramento Valley with severe floods. And
still farther north, at places on the Oregon and
Washington coast, the annual precipitation
reaches very high figures indeed. If one then
returns to the other extreme, in far south-
eastern California, one is altogether in a desert
region. Normally the wet season of central
and southern California, even where the rain-

fall is considerable, is diversified by extended intervals of beautifully fair and mild weather. But nowhere on the Pacific Coast has the variation of seasons the characters customary in the eastern country. A true winter exists, indeed, in the high Sierra, but even here this season has a character very different from that of the New England winter. Enormous falls of snow on the upper Sierra slopes are, indeed, frequent. But on the other hand, there are many places in the Sierra where an early spring very rapidly melts away these masses of snow from the upper foot-hills, and leads by a swift transition to the climate of the California dry season, in a dramatic fashion that happens to be prominent amongst my own childhood memories.

In general, then, in California and Oregon, with the great western ocean so near, the routine of the year's climate is much more definite and predetermined than in our Atlantic states. In western Oregon, where, as we have said, the climate is far more moist, the rains begin about the end of September and continue with more or fewer intermissions until May or June. The dry season then lasts steadily for three or four months. In California the dry season grows longer, the rainy season less persistent and wealthy in watery gifts, the farther south we go, until in the far south, except on the coast, there is often a very short intermission in the year's drought.

So much for the climate of this region as a whole. Meanwhile, there are numerous local varieties, and amongst these more distinctly local influences that modify the climate both in the wet and in the dry seasons, the Coast Range of California plays a very important part. This range, separated, as we have seen, from the Sierra by the Sacramento and San Joaquin valleys, joins its masses with those of the Sierra both at the northern end of the Sacramento Valley and at the southern extremity of the San Joaquin Valley. These two rivers, the Sacramento and the San Joaquin, flowing the one southward and the other northward, join their waters and find an exit to the sea through San Francisco Bay, which itself opens into the ocean through the Golden Gate. The Sacramento Valley is thus bounded on the east by a range that varies in height from seven thousand to fourteen thousand feet. The Coast Range on the west has an elevation varying from two thousand to four thousand, and in some cases rising to five thousand feet. The elevation of the Coast Range is thus sufficient to affect, in the rainy season, the precipitation in some localities, although the greatest rainfalls of the rainy season in California are due to the influence of the Sierra upon the moisture-laden winds of the sea during the passage of the areas of low pressure. But decidedly more marked is the influence of the Coast Range during the summer months, upon the determination of local climate along the northern Californian coast. Here the summer, from Monterey northward, is along the coast decidedly cold, — sea-breezes and frequent mists marking the days of the entire dry season, while at night the winds usually fall, and the cold may not be so severely felt.

But frequently only a few miles will separate these cold regions of the coast from the hot interior of the Sacramento Valley or from the smaller valleys on the eastern slope of the Coast Range.

To sum up the total result of all these conditions, one may say that the main feature of the whole climate, apart from its mildness, is the relatively predictable character of the year's weather. In the dryer regions of the south, wherever irrigation is possible and has been developed, the agriculturist often feels a superiority to weather conditions which makes him rejoice in the very drought that might otherwise be regarded as so formidable. In central California one is sure, in advance, of the weather that will steadily prevail during all the summer months. Agricultural operations are thus rendered definite by the knowledge of when the drought is coming, and by the freedom from all fear of sudden storms during the harvest season.

That this climate is delightful to those who are used to its routine will be well known to most readers. That it is not without its disagreeable features is equally manifest to every tourist. Nor can one say that this far western country is free from decided variations in the fortunes of different years. Where irrigation is not developed, great anxiety is frequently felt with regard to the sufficiency of the annual rain supply of the rainy season. Years of relative flood and of relative drought are as well known here as elsewhere. Nor is one wholly free, within any one season, from unexpected and sometimes disagreeably long-continued periods of unseasonable temperature. A high barometer over the region north and east of California occasionally brings to pass the well-known California "northers." These have, in the rainy season, a character that in some respects reminds one of the familiar cold-wave phenomena of the east, although the effect is very much more moderate. Frosts may then extend throughout northern California, may beset the central Coast Range, and may on occasion extend far into the southern part of California itself.

But when the "northers" come during the dry season, they are frequently intensely hot winds, whose drought, associated with hill or forest fires, may give rise to very memorable experiences. But these are the inevitable and minor vicissitudes of a climate which is, on the whole, remarkably steady, and which is never as trying as are the well-known variations of our own northeastern climate. The generally good effect upon the health of such a climate is modified in certain cases by the possibly overstimulating character of the coast summer, which, as for instance at San Francisco, permits one to work without thought of holidays all the year round. In my own boyhood it used often to be said that there were busy men in San Francisco who had reached that place in 1849, and who had become prominent in mercantile or other city life, and who had never taken vacations, and never left San Francisco even to cross the bay, from the hour of their coming until that moment. Of course, such men can be found in almost any busy community, but these men seemed rather characteristic of the early California days and suggested the way in which a favorable climate may on occasion be misused by an ambitious man to add to the strains otherwise incident to the life of a new country.

If one now turns from the climate to the other aspects of our region, the general topography at once suggests marked features that must needs be of great importance to the entire life of any such country. California and Oregon are sharply sundered from one another by the ranges north of the Sacramento Valley. The Washington region, about Puget Sound, is destined to still a third and decidedly separate life, by reason of its relation to those magnificent inland waters, and by reason of the two high ranges which bound the shores of the American portion of Puget Sound.

And, in fact, the country of the whole Pacific Coast may be regarded as geographically divided into at least four great regions: the Washington region, in the neighborhood of Puget Sound; the Oregon region with the

184

valley of the Columbia; the northern and central California region, including the coast and bay of San Francisco, together with the great interior valley; and, finally, the southern region of California. Both the social development and the material future of these four great sections of the Pacific Coast must always be mutually somewhat distinct and independent. The northern and central California region, the third of those just enumerated, is in possession of the largest harbor between Puget Sound and the southern boundary of the United States. It is, therefore, here that the civilization of the west was destined to find its first centre. Nor can this province ever have a social destiny independent of that of San Francisco itself. The southern California region, while not separated from central and northern California by any very high barrier, is still marked off by certain features due to the amount of precipitation, and to the smaller harbors of this part of the Pacific Coast.

I have already mentioned more than once

the breadth of landscape characteristic especially of central California, but often visible elsewhere on the Pacific Coast. Here is a feature that has to do at once with the materially important and with the topographically interesting features of this land. When you stand on Mount Diablo, a mountain about three thousand eight hundred feet high, and some fifteen miles east of San Francisco Bay, you look in one direction down upon the ocean and upon San Francisco Bay itself, while in the other direction you have in full sight the Sierra Range beyond the great valley, and vast reaches of the interior valley itself. Similarly, from the upper foot-hills of the Sierra, every chance elevation that overtops its neighbors a little gives you far-reaching views of the interior valley. The normally clear air of a great part of the year determines the character and sharp outlines of these broad views. The young Californian is thus early used to a country that, as it were, tells its principal secrets at a glance, and he sometimes finds his eye pained and confused either

by the monotonous landscapes of the prairies
of our middle west, or by the baffling topography of many parts of New England or of
our middle states, where one small valley at
a time invites one to guess what may be its
unseen relations to its neighbors. The effect
of all this breadth and clearness of natural
scenery on mental life cannot be doubted.

III

Of climate and topography this very summary view must now suffice. We turn from
nature toward life, and ask ourselves what
bearing these geographical features have had
upon the still so incomplete social development of California.

In 1846, at the outset of our war with
Mexico, the Mexican province of California
extended toward the interior, at least on
paper, so far as to include the present Nevada
and Utah; but only the California coast itself
was really known to its inhabitants. California was seized by the American fleet at
the outset of the war. Its value to our coun-

try had been earlier made known partly
through the New England traders who dealt
on that coast, and partly through the appearance in the territory of American settlers.
The famous report of the expedition of 1844
made by Lieutenant Fremont brought to a
focus the popular interest in the importance
of the entire territory, and prepared the way
for the excitement aroused by the discovery
of gold in 1848.

The gold excitement determined the entire
future history of California; and here of
course the immediate influence of the physical
upon the social conditions is the best known
fact about the state. The golden period of
California may be regarded as filling all the
years between 1848 and 1860. Or perhaps
a still better dividing line might be made in
the year 1866, when the government first surveyed the mineral lands of California and
parted with its title to these lands, so that
the conditions of mining ownership were
thenceforth no longer primitive. Up to that
time the miners of California had worked by

government consent upon land to which
they could acquire no title, so that their right
to hold land was entirely due to miner's custom and to occupation, both of which were
recognized by the courts of the state in dealing with conflicts amongst miners. With
the close of the distinctively mining period,
begins the agricultural period of California.
Gold mining has of course continued until
the present day, but the development of agriculture soon surpassed in importance that of
all other industries in the state.

Nevertheless, the civilization of the agricultural period has been of course determined in large part, despite the change of
material conditions, by the traditions of the
more romantic golden period. The California pioneers are gradually passing away;
but as the fathers and the early Puritans determined in many respects the future of New
England, so the miners, together with their
peers, the merchants of early San Francisco,
lived a life whose traditions, directly due to
the physical conditions under which they

189

worked, are sure to be of long-continued, perhaps of permanently obvious, influence in the development of the civilization of California.

If one attempts to describe in what way the civilization either of the golden days or of the later agricultural period has been affected by the geographical conditions, a student of my own habits and prejudices feels at once disposed to pass directly to the inner life of the Californian and to ask himself what influence the nature and climate of such a region seem to have upon the life of the individual mind and body, and, indirectly, upon the social order. Here of course one treads upon ground at once fascinating and enormously difficult. Generalization is limited by the fact of great varieties of personal character and type with which we are dealing. But after all, I think that in California literature, in the customary expressions of Californians in speaking to one another, and, to a very limited degree, in the inner consciousness of any one who has grown up in California, we have evidence of certain ways in which the conditions of such a region must influence the life and, I suppose in the end, the character of the whole community. I feel disposed, then, to try to suggest very briefly how it feels to grow up in such a climate, to live in such a region, thus separated by wide stretches of country from other portions of our own land and from the world at large, thus led by the kindliness of nature into a somewhat intimate, even if uncomprehended, relation to the physical conditions, and thus limited to certain horizons in one's experience. I speak of course as a native Californian, but I also do not venture to limit even for a moment my characterization by reference to my own private experience. Californians are rather extraordinarily conscious of the relation between their home and their lives. Newcomers who have grown up elsewhere are constantly comparing their natural surroundings with those that they knew before. The natives, for reasons that I shall suggest in a moment, are put into a relation with nature which, whether they are students of nature or not, and whether they are observant or not, is in feeling a peculiarly intimate relation. The consequence may, as I have already suggested, be best understood by a reference to some of the wealthy and varied literature that California has already produced.

Every one is familiar with that reflection of the change of seasons in poetical literature which we find first in the classic English literature, which we find again gradually appearing in new forms in adaptation to the more special conditions of our American climate. New England nature has now been perhaps almost too frequently characterized in literary art. We are here to ask how the nature of California comes to be characterized. Let me appeal at once to some of the poets to tell us.

The most familiar account of the California climate in literature is Bret Harte's characterization of the seasonal changes in his poem, "Concepcion Argüello." The scene is here

192

at the Presidio at San Francisco, close by the Golden Gate, where the heroine waited for her lover during the long years that the poem describes.

" Day by day on wall and bastion beat the hollow empty breeze —
  Day by day the sunlight glittered on the vacant, smiling seas;
  Week by week the near hills whitened in their dusty leather cloaks —
  Week by week the far hills darkened from the fringing plain of oaks;
  Till the rains came, and far-breaking, on the fierce south-wester tost,
  Dashed the whole long coast with color, and then vanished and were lost.
  So each year the seasons shifted, wet and warm and drear and dry;
  Half a year of clouds and flowers — half a year of dust and sky."

The nature which is thus depicted has of course many other aspects besides this its fundamental rhythm; but prominent in all the literary descriptions is the stress laid upon the coming of the rains, — an event which occupies, very naturally, the same place in

o   193

the California poet's mind that the spring
occupies elsewhere. Only what this spring-
time breaks in upon in California is not in
general cold, but drought. It is here not the
bursting away of any iron barrier of frost,
but the clearing of the hazy air, the introduction of a rich and sudden new life, the re-
moving of a dull and dry oppression from the
heart, — it is such things that first come to
mind when one views this change. A student of the University of California in the
year 1878, a lady who has won success in more
than one branch of literature, Miss Millicent
Shinn, published in a college paper of that
time the following sonnet, under the title of
"Rain." The poem deserves to be recalled
here, just as a suggestion of the relation
between nature and the individual mind
under such conditions : —

> "It chanced me once that many weary weeks
>   I walked to daily work across a plain,
>   Far-stretching, barren since the April rain;
>   And now, in gravelly beds of vanished creeks,
>   November walked dry shod. On every side

Round the horizon hung a murky cloud, —
No hills, no waters; and above that shroud
A wan sky rested shadowless and wide.
Until one night came down the earliest rain;
And in the morning, lo, in fair array,
Blue ranges crowned with snowy summits, lay
All round about the fair transfigured plain.
    Oh, would that such a rain might melt away
    In tears the cloud that chokes my heart with pain."

The heavy air of the close of the dry season, the weary waiting for the autumn rains, the quick change as the new life came, — all these things bring characteristically before one the nature life of central California, — a region of the half-arid type, where the conditions are far enough from true desert conditions, while at moments they simulate the latter. Yet not merely this fundamental rhythm of the climate so easily impressive to every sojourner, arouses the sensitive attention of the life-long inhabitant. The dwellers by the shores of San Francisco Bay see these seasonal changes in the midst of a highly varied landscape. From the hill slopes on the eastern shores of that great harbor one looks toward the Golden Gate. North of the Gate rise the rugged heights of Mount Tamalpais, to a point about twenty-six hundred feet above the sea level. South of the Gate, San Francisco itself adds its smoke to the ocean mists, and its hilly summits to the generally bold landscape. The wide expanse of water, stretching north and south in the bay, changes color under the daylight in the most varied manner, according as cloud and sunshine, or as dawn, morning, afternoon, and sunset pass before you. In the summertime the afternoon ocean mists enter, along with the steadily rising daily wind which falls only with the twilight. One of California's most successful poets, Miss Coolbrith, depicts this scene in her poem entitled "Two Pictures."

MORNING

> "As in a quiet dream,
>   The mighty waters seem:
>   Scarcely a ripple shows
>   Upon their blue repose.

196

THE PACIFIC COAST

The sea-gulls smoothly ride
Upon the drowsy tide,
And a white sail doth sleep
Far out upon the deep.

A dreamy purple fills
The hollows of the hills;
A single cloud floats through
The sky's serenest blue;

And far beyond the Gate,
The massed vapors wait —
White as the walls that ring
The City of the King.

There is no sound, no word;
Only a happy bird
Trills to her nestling young,
A little, sleepy song.

This is the holy calm;
The heavens dropping balm;
The Love made manifest,
And near; the perfect rest.

EVENING

The day grows wan and cold:
In through the Gate of Gold
The restless vapors glide,
Like ghosts upon the tide.

The brown bird folds her wing,
Sad, with no song to sing.
Along the streets the dust
Blows sharp, with sudden gust.

The night comes, chill and gray;
Over the sullen bay,
What mournful echoes pass
From lonely Alcatraz!

O bell, with solemn toll,
As for a passing soul!
As for a soul that waits,
In vain, at heaven's gates.

This is the utter blight;
The sorrow infinite
Of earth; the closing wave;
The parting, and the grave."

Such is the daily drama of the dry season
at the bay. On the other hand, the rainy
season itself contains some tragedies that in
no wise belong to the eastern winter. There
are the northers, with their periods of relative
chill and their swift winged sternness; and
these northers have often been celebrated in
California verse. But apart from such colder

periods, the loud roaring storms and heavy
rains are often likely to stand in a curious
contrast to the abounding life of vegetation
which the rains themselves have aroused. It
is possible to cultivate roses in one's garden
throughout the greater part of the year.
These, the rainy season will generally encourage in their blooming. On the other hand,
the stormy wind will from time to time de-
stroy them with its own floods of cruelty.
Miss Coolbrith depicts such a scene in the
poem entitled, "My 'Cloth of Gold.'" As
in tropical countries, so here the long storms
seem often much darker and drearier by
reason of their warfare with the rich life
amidst which they rage.

IV

Such are a few of the many instances that
might be given of the emotional reactions of
sensitive minds in the presence of California
nature. But now the outer aspect of nature
unquestionably moulds both the emotions
and the customs of mankind, insensibly af-

fects men's temperaments in ways which, as
we know, somehow or other tend to become
hereditary, however we may view the vexed
question concerning the heredity of acquired
characters. Moreover, the influence of nature
upon custom which every civilization depicts,
is precisely the kind of influence that from
moment to moment expresses itself psychologically in the more typical emotions of sensitive souls. Thus, one may observe that if
we are considering the relation between civilization and climate, and are endeavoring to
speculate in however vague a manner upon
the future of a society in a given environment,
we may well turn to the poets, not for a solution of our problem, but for getting significant hints. Or, to put the case somewhat
boldly otherwise, I should say that the vast
processes which in the course of centuries
appear in the changes of civilization due to
climate, involve, as it were, tremendously
complex mathematical functions. If it were
possible for us to state these stupendous
functions, we should be possessed of the secret

of such social changes. Of such a stupendous function, a group of poems, expressing as they do momentary human changes, might be called, if you like, a system of partial, and I admit very partial, differential equations. I do not hope to integrate any such system of equations, or to gain an exact view of the types of the functions from a consideration of them, and of course I admit with readiness that I am using only a very rough mathematical metaphor. But to translate the matter once more into literal terms, the tendencies of the moment are in their way indications of what the tendencies of the ages are to be.

Now what all this poetry in general psychologically means, quite apart from special moods, is that the Californian, of necessity, gains a kind of sensitiveness to nature which is different in type from the sensitiveness that a severer climate would inevitably involve, and different too in type from that belonging to climates mild but moist and more variable. In the first piace, as you see, such a climate permits one to be a great deal out of doors in the midst of nature. It permits wide views, where the outlines are vast and in general clear. As, when you are on a steamer it is a matter of some skill to understand what are the actual conditions of wind and sea, while, when you are on a sailing vessel you constantly feel both the wind and the sea with a close intimacy that needs no technical knowledge to make it at least appreciated, so, in the case of such a climate as the one of California, your relations with nature are essentially intimate, whether you are a student of nature or not. Your dependence upon nature you feel in one sense more, and in another sense less, — more, because you are more constantly in touch with the natural changes of the moment; less, because you know that nature is less to be feared than under severer conditions. And this intimacy with nature means a certain change in your relations to your fellow-men. You get a sense of power from these wide views, a habit of personal independence from the contemplation of a world that the eye seems to own. Especially in country life the individual Californian consequently tends toward a certain kind of independence which I find in a strong and subtle contrast to the sort of independence that, for instance, the New England farmer cultivates. The New England farmer must fortify himself in his stronghold against the seasons. He must be ready to adapt himself to a year that permits him to prosper only upon decidedly hard terms. But the California country proprietor can have, during the drought, more leisure, unless, indeed, his ambition for wealth too much engrosses him. His horses are plenty and cheap. His fruit crops thrive easily. He is able to supply his table with fewer purchases, with less commercial dependence. His position is, therefore, less that of the knight in his castle and more that of the free dweller in the summer cottage, who is indeed not at leisure, but can easily determine how he shall be busy. It is of little importance to him who his next neighbor is. At pleasure he can ride or drive a good way to find his friends; can choose, like the southern planter of former days, his own range of hospitality; can devote himself, if a man of cultivation, to reading during a good many hours at his own choice, or, if a man of sport, can find during a great part of the year easy opportunities for hunting or for camping both for himself and for the young people of his family. In the dry season he knows beforehand what engagements can be made, without regard to the state of the weather, since the state of the weather is predetermined.

The free life and interchange of hospitality, so often described in the accounts of early California, has left its traces in the country life of California at the present day. Very readily, if you have moderate means, you can create your own quiet estate at a convenient distance from the nearest town. You may cover your house with a bower of roses, surround yourself with an orchard, quickly grow eucalyptus as a shade tree, and with nearly equal facility multiply other shade trees. You become, on easy terms, a pro-

prietor, with estate and home of your own.
Now all this holds, in a sense, of any mild climate. But in California the more regular
routine of wet and dry seasons modifies and
renders more stable the general psychological
consequences. All this is encouraging to a
kind of harmonious individuality that already
tends in the best instances toward a somewhat Hellenic type.

A colleague of my own, a New Englander
of the strictest persuasion, who visited California for a short time when he was himself
past middle life, returned enthusiastic with
the report that the California countrymen
seemed to him to resemble the ancient, yes,
even the Homeric, Greeks of the Odyssey.
The Californians had their independence of
judgment; their carelessness of what a bar-
barian might think, so long as he came from
beyond the border; their apparent freedom
in choosing what manner of men they should
be; their ready and confident speech. All
these things my friend at once noticed as
characteristic. Thus different in type are

these country proprietors from the equally individual, the secretively independent, the silently conscientious New England villagers. They are also quite different from the typical southern proprietors. From the latter they differ in having less tendency to respect traditions, and in laying much less stress upon formal courtesies. The Californian, like the westerner in general, is likely to be somewhat abrupt in speech, and his recent coming to the land has made him on the whole quite indifferent to family tradition. I myself, for instance, reached twenty years of age without ever becoming clearly conscious of what was meant by judging a man by his antecedents, a judgment that in an older and less isolated community is natural and inevitable, and that, I think, in most of our western communities, grows up more rapidly than it has grown up in California, where the geographical isolation is added to the absence of tradition. To my own mind, in childhood, every human being was, with a few exceptions, whatever he happened to be. Hereditary distinctions I appreciated only in case of four types of humanity. There were the Chinamen, there were the Irishmen, there were the Mexicans, and there were the rest of us. Within each of these types, every man, to my youthful mind, was precisely what God and himself had made him, and it was distinctly a new point of view to attach a man to the antecedents that either his family or his other social relationships had determined for him. Now, I say, this type of individuality, known more or less in our western communities, but developed in peculiarly high degree in California, seems to me due not merely to the newness of the community, and not merely to that other factor of geographical isolation that I just mentioned, but to the relation with nature of which we have already spoken. It is a free and on the whole an emotionally exciting, and also as we have said, an engrossing and intimate relation.

In New England, if you are moody, you may wish to take a long walk out-of-doors, but that is not possible at all or even at most seasons. Nature may not be permitted to comfort you. In California, unless you are afraid of the rain, nature welcomes you at almost any time. The union of the man and the visible universe is free, is entirely unchecked by any hostility on the part of nature, and is such as easily fills one's mind with wealth of warm experience. Our poets just quoted have laid stress upon the directly or symbolically painful aspects of the scene. But these are sorrows of a sort that mean precisely that relation with nature which I am trying to characterize, not the relation of hostility but of closeness. And this is the sort of closeness determined not merely by mild weather, but by long drought and by the relative steadiness of all the climatic conditions.

Now, I must feel that such tendencies are of vast importance, not merely to-day but for all time. They are tendencies whose moral significance in the life of California is of course both good and evil, since man's relations with nature are, in general, a neutral material upon which ethical relations may be based. If you are industrious, this intimacy with nature means constant coöperation, a coöperation never interrupted by frozen ground and deep snow. If you tend to idleness, nature's kindliness may make you all the more indolent, and indolence is a possible enough vice with the dwellers in all mild climates. If you are morally careless, nature encourages your freedom, and tends in so far to develop a kind of morale frequently characteristic of the dwellers in gentle climates. Yet the nature of California is not enervating. The nights are cool, even in hot weather; owing to the drought the mildness of the air is not necessarily harmful. Moreover, the nature that is so uniform also suggests in a very dignified way a regularity of existence, a definite reward for a definitely planned deed. Climate and weather are at their best always capricious, and, as we have seen, the variations of the California seasons have involved the farmers in much anxiety, and in many cases have given the farming business, as carried on in certain California communities, the same sort of gambling tendency that originally vitiated the social value of the mining industry. But on the other hand, as the conditions grew more stable, as agriculture developed, vast irrigation enterprises introduced once more a conservative tendency. Here again for the definite deed nature secures a definite return. In regions subject to irrigation, man controls the weather as he cannot elsewhere. He is independent of the current season. And this tendency to organization — a tendency similar to the one that was obviously so potent in the vast ancient civilization of Egypt, — is present under Californian conditions, and will make itself felt.

Individuality, then, but of a peculiar type, and a tendency despite all this individualism toward agricultural conservatism and a definite social organization — these are already the results of this climate.

V

I have spoken already several times of the

geographical isolation of this region. This has been a factor that was felt of course in the social life from the very outset, and more in the early days than at present. To be sure, it was never without its compensating features. It shows its influences in a way that varies with pretty definite periods of California history. In the earliest days, before the new-comers in California supposed that agriculture was possible on any large scale, nearly everything was imported. Butter, for instance, was sent around the Horn to San Francisco. And throughout the early years most of the population felt, so to speak, morally rooted in the eastern communities from which they had sprung. This tendency retarded for a long time the development of California society, and made the pioneers careless as to the stability of their social structure; encouraged corrupt municipal administration in San Francisco; gave excuse for the lynching habit in the hastily organized mining communities. But a reaction quickly came. After the general good order which as a fact characterized the year 1849 had gradually given place, with the increase of population, to the disorders of 1851 and to the municipal errors of the years between 1850 and 1856 in the city of San Francisco, there came a period of reform and of growing conservatism which marked all the time of the later mining period and of the transition to the agricultural period. During these years many who had come to California without any permanent purpose decided to become members of the community, and decided in consequence to create a community of which it was worth while to be a member. The consequence was the increase of the influence of the factor of geographical isolation in its social influence upon the life of California. The community became self-conscious, independent, indisposed to take advice from without, very confident of the future of the state and of the boundless prosperity soon to be expected; and within the years between 1860 and 1870 a definite local tradition of California life was developed upon the basis of the memories and characters that had been formed in the early days. The consequence was a provincial California, whose ideals at last assumed that form of indifference to the barbarians beyond the border which my friend noticed as surviving even to the time of the visit of which I have spoken.

But the completion of the transcontinental railway in 1869 introduced once more the factor of physical connection with the East, and of commercial rivalry with the investors of the Mississippi Valley who now undertook, along with the capitalists of California, to supply the mining population of the still newer Rocky Mountain regions. On the whole, I should say that for a good while the provincial California, in the rather extremer sense of the tradition of the sixties and early seventies, held its own against the influence of the railway. But the original railway did not remain alone. Other transcontinental lines developed. The southern portion of the state, long neglected during the early days, became, in the beginning of the eighties, the theatre of a new immigration and of a new and on the whole decidedly more eastern civilization. There has resulted since that time a third stage of California life and society, a stage marked by a union of the provincial independence of the middle period with the complex social influences derived from the East and from the world at large. The California of to-day is still the theatre of the struggle of these opposing forces.

VI

It remains necessary to characterize more fully the way in which the consequences of the early days, joined to the geographical factors upon which we have already laid stress, have influenced the problems of California life and society. From the very outset, climate and geographical position, and the sort of life in which men were engaged, have encouraged types of individuality whose subtle distinction from those elsewhere to be found we have already attempted in a very inadequate fashion to suggest. Accordingly,

from the first period down to the present
time, the California community has been a
notable theatre for the display of political
and financial, and, on occasion, of intellectual
individuality of decidedly extraordinary
types. The history of both earlier and later
California politics has been a very distinctly
personal history. The political life of the
years before the war had as their most picturesque incident the long struggle for the
United States Senatorship carried on between
David Broderick and William Gwin. This
contest involved personalities far more than
principles. Gwin and Broderick were both
of them extremely picturesque figures, —
the one a typical Irish-American, the other a
Southerner. The story of their bitter warfare
is a familiar California romance. The tragic
death of Broderick, in duel with the once
notorious Terry, is a tale that long had a decidedly national prominence. Terry himself is an example of a type of individuality
not elsewhere unknown in border life, but
developed under peculiarly Californian con-

ditions. Terry was, very frankly, a man of blood. Regarding him as a man of blood, one finds him in many ways, and within his own limits, an interesting, even a conscientious and attractive personality. He was at one time upon the Supreme Bench of the state of California. He warred with the Vigilance Committee of 1856 in a manner that certainly wins one's respect for his skill in bringing that organization into a very difficult position. He carried on this warfare both as judge of the Supreme Court and as wielder of a bowie knife. When he slew Broderick, he did so in a fashion that, so far as the duelling code permitted, was perfectly fair. He lived for years with a disposition to take the unpopular side of every question, to fight bitterly for causes for which no other man cared, and it was precisely for such a cause that he finally died. His attempted assault upon Judge Field, and the controversy that led thereto, and that resulted in Terry's death, was, a few years since, in everybody's memory.

216

It would be wholly wrong to conceive California individuality as at all fairly represented by a border type such as Terry's. Yet when one looks about in California society and politics, one finds even at the present day picturesque personalities preserving their picturesqueness amidst various grades of nobility and baseness, in a fashion more characteristic, I think, than is customary in most of our newer communities. The nobler sort of picturesque personality may be the public benefactor, like Lick or Sutro. He may be the social reformer of vast ideals, like Henry George. Or again the baser individual may be the ignorant demagogue of the grade of Dennis Kearney. Your California hero may be the chief of the Vigilance Committee of 1856, or some other typical and admired pioneer, growing old in the glory of remembered early deeds. He may be the railway magnate, building a transcontinental line under all sorts of discouragements, winning a great fortune, and dying just as he founds a university. But in all these phases he remains

217

the strong individual type of man that in a great democracy is always necessary. It is just this type that, as some of us fear, the conditions of our larger democracy in more eastern regions tend far too much to eliminate. In California, such individuality is by no means yet eliminated.

There is a symptom of this fact which I have frequently noted, both while I was a continuous resident of California and from time to time since. Individualistic communities are almost universally, and paradoxically enough, communities that are extremely cruel to individuals. It is so in a debating club, where individuality is encouraged, but where every speaker is subject to fierce criticism. Now, this is still so in California to an extent which surprises even one who is used to the public controversies of some of our eastern cities. The individual who, by public action or utterance, rises above the general level in California, is subject to a kind of attack which strong men frequently enjoy, but which even the stranger finds on occasion peculiarly

merciless. That absence of concern for a
man's antecedents of which I before spoke,
contributes to this very mercilessness. A
friend once remarked to me that in California,
Phillips Brooks, had he appeared there before
reaching the very height of his reputation,
would have had small chance to win a hearing,
so little reverence would have been felt for
the mere form of the causes that he maintained.
This remark was perhaps unfair, since a
stranger preacher — Thomas Starr King,
— gained in early California days, at about
the beginning of the war, a very great public
reputation in a short time, received great
sympathy, and had a mighty influence. But,
on the other hand, it is perfectly certain that
the public man who intends to maintain his
ideals in California will have to do so under
fire, and will have to be strong enough to
bear the fire. His family, or the clubs to
which he belongs, the university that he repre-
sents, the church that supports him, — none of
these factors will in such a community easily
determine his standing. He works in a commu-

nity where the pioneer tradition still remains, — the tradition of independence and of distrust toward enthusiasm. For one feels in California, very keenly, that enthusiasm may after all mean sham, until one is quite sure that it has been severely tested. And this same community, so far as its country population is concerned, is made up of persons who, whether pioneers or newcomers, live in the aforesaid agricultural freedom, in easy touch with nature, not afraid of the sentiments of the crowd, although of course disposed, like other human beings, to be affected by a popular cry in so far as it attacks men or declares new ideals insignificant. It is much more difficult to arouse the enthusiastic sympathy of such people than it is, in case one has the advantage of the proper social backing, to affect the public opinion of a more highly organized social order in a less isolated region.

And now we have seen the various ways in which this sort of individuality is a product of the natural features of the state as well as of those early conditions which themselves were determined by geographical factors. On the other hand, in addition to this prevalence of individuality and this concomitant severity of the judgment of prominent individuals, there are social conditions characteristic of San Francisco which can also be referred to geographical and climatic factors. Early in the development of San Francisco a difficulty in the education of the young appeared which, as I fancy, has not yet been removed. This difficulty had to do with the easy development of vagrancy in city children. Vagrancy is a universal evil of cities, but the California vagrant can easily pass the night out-doors during the greater part of the year. A friend of mine who was connected with the management of San Francisco public schools for a number of years, laid stress upon this climatic factor and its dangers in official communications published at the time of his office. The now too well-known name of "hoodlum" originated in San Francisco, and is said to have been the name adopted by a particular group of young men. The social complications of the time of the sand-lot, when Dennis Kearney led laborers into a dangerous pass, were again favored by climatic conditions. Public meetings out-of-doors and in the sand-lot could be held with a certain freedom and persistency in California that would be impossible without interruption elsewhere. While such factors have nothing to do with discontent, they greatly increase the opportunities for agitation. The new constitution of California, adopted in 1879, was carried at the polls by a combination of the working men of San Francisco with the dissatisfied farmers of the interior. This dissatisfaction of the farmers was no doubt due in the main to the inadequacy of their comprehension of the material conditions under which they were working. The position of California — its geographical isolation again — has been one complicating factor for the California farmer, since luxuriant nature easily furnished him, in case he should use wise methods, with a rich supply, while his geographical isolation made access to market somewhat difficult. This difficulty about the markets long affected California political life in the form of dissatisfaction felt against the railway, which was of course held responsible and which in fact for years was more or less responsible for an increase of these difficulties of reaching the market. Well, this entire series of complications, which in 1879 combined San Francisco working men with the farmers of the interior, and changed the constitution of the state, is an example of the complex way in which the geographical situation and the factors of climate have acted to affect social movements.

On the other hand, the individuality aforesaid, when brought into the presence of such social agitations, has frequently proved in California life a conservative factor of great importance. The mob may be swept away for a time by an agitating idea. But the individual Californian himself is suspicious of mobs. The agitations in question proved transient. Even the constitution, designed to give the discontented whatever they most supposed they wanted, proved to be susceptible of a very conservative construction by the courts, and public opinion in California has never been very long under the sway of any one illusion. The individuality that we have described quickly revolts against its false prophets. In party politics, California proves to be an extremely doubtful state. Party ties are not close. The vote changes from election to election. The independent voter is well in place. Finally, through all these tendencies, there runs a certain idealism, often more or less unconscious. This idealism is partly due to the memory of the romance due to the unique marvels of the early days. It is also sustained by precisely that intimacy with nature which renders the younger Californians so sensitive. I think that perhaps Edward Rowland Sill, whose poems are nowadays so widely appreciated, has given the most representative expression to the resulting spirit of California, to that tension between individualism and loyalty, between shrewd conservatism and bold radicalism, which marks this community.

V

SOME RELATIONS OF PHYSICAL TRAINING TO THE PRESENT PROBLEMS OF MORAL EDUCATION IN AMERICA

V

SOME RELATIONS OF PHYSICAL TRAINING TO THE PRESENT PROBLEMS OF MORAL EDUCATION IN AMERICA [1]

IN asking me to address this Society, your Secretary was well aware that I have no right and no desire to pass judgment upon any of the more technical problems which are peculiar to the profession of physical education. But there are problems which are common to your profession and to that region of inquiry to which I am most devoted. These common problems, in fact, interest all who are concerned in the welfare of humanity, and who in particular aim to further the welfare of our country. I refer to those problems of moral education which, in the present time, assume new and difficult forms in American life. I am well aware that those of you, and of your numerous colleagues, who have been most

[1] An address before the Boston Physical Education Association.

229

earnest in furthering the cause of physical education, not only in our land, but in Europe, have always laid great stress upon the close relation of sound physical training to good moral training. And we all know how, from primitive times, mankind have used various forms of physical exercise as a part of the discipline which tribes or, later, nations or, in our modern days, civilized men generally, have regarded as fitted to form whatever well-rounded types of individual character the various stages of human culture have admired. Physical training has repeatedly had, in the past, a place in the religious life of various peoples, and systems of secular training have often so much the more followed analogous lines. Chivalry in Europe, Bushido in Japan, were systems of conduct which were inseparable from various plans for physical training. To-day most of you lay constant stress upon your function, not only as teachers who care for the health, for the physical growth, and for the accompanying intellectual development of your pupils, but as instructors who contribute what you all believe to be a very significant part of the moral education of the youth of the country. The social organizations known as Young Men's Christian Associations are the expression of explicitly religious motives, and are unquestionably intended for an ethical purpose. But they regard their gymnasiums as an essential part of their work. And this is but one example of the recognition of a close linkage between physical and moral training, — a linkage which you all believe to be important, and which most of you consciously emphasize in your own practice.

The problems of moral education are common, then, to you and to your colleagues in other branches of education, of inquiry, and of social work. I myself, as a teacher of philosophy, have lately been led to consider some of the problems of ethics with especial reference to the present state of our American civilization. I have supposed, therefore, that you might be interested if I now attempt to state some of these problems in a way to suggest their possible connections with your profession. I make these suggestions very tentatively. As a student of philosophy, I have, indeed, my rights as an inquirer into ethical questions. But, when I try to tell you my view about how some of these questions relate to your calling, I at once run the risks which any man runs who attempts to connect his own views with those of others, by appealing to his fellows regarding the matters in which they are expert while he is not expert. But, in any case, I shall try to keep to the ground that is common to your calling and to mine. You all of you are interested in what some of you may call the philosophy of physical training. I am professionally concerned with philosophy. And so I want to meet you upon this common basis of your interest and mine in the questions which concern what I may call the moral philosophy of your calling.

I

I shall begin by asking what we mean by the moral training of an individual man.

This question we can best attempt to answer by sketching a moral ideal, — an ideal of what, as I suppose, we all, more or less consciously, desire any moral agent to become. If we define this ideal, then the moral training of an individual will be defined as the training that is best adapted to help that individual to approach this moral ideal.

The ideal human moral agent, as I assert, is a man who is *whole-heartedly and effectively loyal to some fitting object of loyalty.* This first statement of the moral ideal may seem vague to you. I hasten to explain a little more precisely what I mean.

I have chosen the good old word " loyal " as the word best adapted to arouse, with the fewest misleading associations, that idea of the moral life which I believe to be rationally the most defensible. But, of course, my own usage of the word " loyal " must attempt to be more exact than the traditional usage is, because such popular words are always applied somewhat recklessly; and the loyalty that I have in mind when I employ this term is something that I try to conceive in as exact a fashion as the subject permits. " Loyalty," as popularly understood, has always meant a certain attitude of mind which faithful friends, lovers, soldiers, or retainers, or which martyrs dying for their faith have exemplified. Plainly, a good many different sorts of people and of deeds have been called loyal. And, if you view the matter merely upon the basis of a comparison of a few widely various instances of loyalty, you may be disposed to say that the moral quality in question is too wavering and confused a feature of character to be fitly used as a type of all moral excellence. Cannot robbers be loyal to their band, slaves to their master, mischievous boys to the comrades whose pranks they incite and applaud, but whose names they refuse to tell to any teacher? Is loyalty, then, always a trait of the morally wise or of the good? Is it a typical virtue? Is it not rather an accidental accompaniment of goodness or, at best, a special form which goodness may sometimes take?

I answer that all these just-mentioned instances of loyalty — even the loyalty of the robber to his band — involve some morally good features. My own definition of loyalty as a fundamental virtue is intended, first to emphasize these good features, which even the blindest forms of loyalty exemplify, then to separate these good features from their accidental setting, and then to define the ideal toward which all the forms of loyalty seem to me to tend. I will therefore proceed at once to characterize loyalty as it appears in its most typical instances and on higher levels.

Loyalty, as I view the essence of this trait, means, in the first place, a certain attitude of mind which we can best understand by considering cases of strong and hearty loyalty as they occur in the life of a mature and highly trained man. This loyal attitude makes a man give himself to the active service of a cause. This cause is one which the loyal man regards, at the moment of action, as something beyond his own private self, and as larger than this private self, as vaster and worthier than any of his private interests. And yet, for the loyal man, his whole private self meanwhile seems inspired by the cause, so that, while he is engaged in his loyal activity, his eyes, his ears, his tongue, his hand, his whole strength, exist, for the time, simply as the organs of his loyalty. When a man is loyal and is actively engaged in his loyal undertakings, he is keenly and clearly conscious, therefore, of a strong contrast, and yet of an equally strong unity, present in his life and in his deeds. He himself, the natural man, with his desires and his private interests, with his muscles and his sense organs, with his property and his powers, — he is there in the world, and he knows this natural self of his, he is definitely aware of it. For loyalty is never mere self-forgetfulness; it is self-devotion. And you cannot devote yourself unless you are aware of yourself. The loyal man lives intensely, vigorously, personally; and over against this natural self of his is his cause, — his side in a game, his army in combat, his country in danger, or perhaps his friend, his beloved, his family, humanity, God. He is conscious of this cause; and so the cause is, in great part, sharply contrasted with this private self of his. It is outside of him, — something vast, dignified, imposing, compelling, objective. Were he not aware of this sharp contrast between himself and his cause, he could not be loyal; for without the contrast the whole affair would be merely one of his private interests and passions. The cause meanwhile is itself no mere thing amongst things. It has at least the value of a person or of a system of persons. It is always, in fact, for any deeply loyal man, something which is at once personal and superpersonal, as your family and your country are for you. One cannot be loyal to merely inanimate things as such. And yet, on the other hand, loyalty always views persons in their deeper relations to something that seems larger than any one human personality or than any mere collection of persons can be. Thus your family is, for your family loyalty, more than the mere collection of its members; and the Joseph of the story was loyal to his brotherly and to his filial ties, and not merely to the various individual brethren.

Well, this contrast of the natural man and of his imposing and objective cause is a fact of which the loyal man is keenly conscious. Yet, despite this fact, he is just as conscious that by his deeds he is always reducing his contrast ever afresh to unity. So long as he is indeed active, wide-awake, effectively loyal, he exists only as servant of this cause. The cause, then, is not only another than his private self; it is in a sense his larger self. Despite the contrast he becomes one with it through his every loyal deed. His private self is its willing instrument. The cause inspires him, acts through him. Loyalty is a sort of possession. It has a demonic force which controls the wayward private self. The cause takes hold of the man, and his organism is no longer his own, so long as the loyal inspiration is upon him.

Such, I say, is, in the briefest language,

a general characterization of the characteristic loyal attitude as it exists in its strong
and maturely developed forms, and especially
in the moments of our effectively loyal conduct.
The boys, loyal to their mates, have the beginnings of loyalty, often in evanescent forms.
The simple-minded folk who do not reflect
are not always so keenly conscious of their
loyalty as more thoughtful folk may be; but
all the more are they able to prove their
loyalty by their deeds. The fully mature and
reflectively devoted man knows his loyalty,
and is possessed by it.

For loyalty, as you see, is essentially an
active virtue. It involves manifold sentiments, — love, good-will, earnestness, delight in the cause; but it is complete only in
motor terms, never in merely sentimental
terms. It is useless to call my feelings loyal unless my muscles somehow express this loyalty.
For my objective cause and my inner private
self, in case I am loyal, are sharply contrasted.
I have to think of both of them, if I am to be
loyal; but they must be brought into unity.

Only my deeds can accomplish this result. My loyal sentiments, if left to themselves, would merely emphasize the contrast without giving life any acceptable unity. Loyal is that loyally does. Hence the loyal attitude is one which especially interests any teacher who is concerned with what his pupil does. The nature of loyalty, then, in the pupil should interest any teacher of physical training who is considerate of the moral aspects of his calling. To be sure, on its higher levels, — in its ideal expressions, — loyalty goes over into regions where mere physical training seems to be very remote from the forms of loyalty that are in question. For loyalty, as I hold, includes in its spirit whatever has been meant in the past by the various inner virtues of sentiment, by charity, by high-mindedness, by spiritual training. It includes these virtues because the loyal act needs and expresses the loyal sentiment. But loyalty combines the sentiments with all the active virtues, — with courage, with patience, with moral initiative, — according as these are needed in one situation or in another. Yet on even its highest levels loyalty has its physical expression. For one is loyal through his deed. If I were here to define the moral ideal in terms of the Pauline virtue of charity, as described in the thirteenth chapter of First Corinthians, we should have indeed some difficulty in pointing out within the limits of this paper the various intermediate steps by which this lofty spiritual virtue of the apostle is linked, as of course it is indeed linked, with the motor activities whereby our organism expresses our will. But, when I now define the moral ideal directly in terms of the loyal attitude, you all see at once how nobody can be effectively loyal unless he is highly trained on the motor side, and unless his ideas and his moral sentiments have long since won their way to an elaborate expression in the deeds of his organism. And so it is indeed plain that surely one way, at least, to prepare a man for a loyal life, is to give him a careful and extended motor training, such as organizes his conduct in harmony with his nobler sentiments. This you all see; and you know that the Japanese long ago saw it also, so that an essential part of their training in Bushido — that is, in their ancient code of chivalrous loyalty — was a training in the physical arts of a Samurai. Our very first view of loyalty suggests then a sense in which physical and moral training may be closely related. But before we estimate what this relation means we must get a fuller notion of what loyalty itself means.

II

I have so far only characterized the general attitude of the higher types of loyalty. Loyalty such as has now been defined may of course take countless special forms. And these forms may appear to be in conflict with one another. In practice the expressions of loyalty do in fact often conflict with one another. The loyal are often quarrelsome. Men can be equally devoted servants of their various causes and yet pass their lives in trying to kill one another. But, since I have so far emphasized the central significance of loyalty as a moral ideal, you may well wonder whether I am indeed right to make loyalty thus central. And so you may well ask me what I have to say, as a moralist, regarding those conflicts of loyalty of which so large a part of the history of mankind has consisted. When equally loyal people are found fighting together, when the heroic devotion of all that a man has and is to the cause which he has chosen as his own appears to demand of him that he should fight and perhaps slay his fellow-man, — well, as you may next ask, in such cases, Who is right? And, if loyalty is indeed any guide to right conduct, why should loyalty counsel me, as it so often seems to do, to oppose and to condemn the loyalty of my fellow? Must there not then be some higher moral principle than that of loyalty, — some principle in terms of which we can find out who is right when two forms of loyalty contradict each other's claims, while each pretends to be the only true loyalty? After all, — as you may insist, — have I shown in the foregoing why the robber ought not to be loyal to his band? Have I shown what wise loyalty is as distinguished from slavish or base loyalty? Have not countless crimes been committed in the name of loyalty?

To such questions I at once answer that, in making loyalty central as a moral principle, I mean to define loyalty in a sense which in the end will make explicit what the true and implied meaning of all loyalty is, even in the cases where loyalty, like love in the proverb, is blind. I defined the loyal attitude as something characteristic of a certain type of personal life. I have said that the genuinely moral attitude is always one of loyalty. I have meant, and I shall indeed stoutly insist, that nobody has reached any morally ideal position who is not, in his more active life, loyal to some cause or to some system of causes. I maintain that without loyalty there is no thoroughgoing morality; and I also insist that all special virtues and duties, such as those which the names benevolence, truthfulness, justice, spirituality, charity, recall to our minds, are parts or are special forms of loyalty. My theory is that the whole moral law is implicitly bound up in the one precept: *Be loyal.* But I freely admit that many men who have been enthusiastically and effectively loyal to various causes, and who in their personal lives have won as mature a notion of loyalty as they were capable of getting, have nevertheless often committed, in the name of loyalty, great crimes. And you may well ask how I explain this fact. You may well wonder how loyalty can be a central moral principle, when lives that were as loyal as the men in question knew how to make them have often been morally mischievous lives.

My answer is that our loyalty leads us into moral error only in so far as we are indeed often blind to what the principle of loyalty actually means and requires. And such blindness is, as men go, human enough and common enough. The corrective to such errors, however, is not the introduction of some other moral principle than that of loyalty, but is just the discovery of the internal meaning, the true sense of the loyal principle itself.

Whoever is loyal loves loyalty for its own sake. Let him merely bethink him of what this love for loyalty means, and he will be led to that definition of the precept: *Be loyal,* — to that definition, I say, which gives to this principle its true scope.

Loyalty, namely, is a common good, — I might say that it is *the* common good of morally trained mankind. This, however, does not mean that all men ought to define in the same monotonous terms the causes to which they are to be loyal. There is a diversity of causes. There is one spirit of loyalty. In the spirit of loyalty, viewed just as a personal attitude, lies the only universal solution of the problem of every private personality. What am I here for? So a man may ask himself. And the rational answer is: You are here to become absorbed in a devotion to some cause or system of causes. Your devotion must be as thorough as your effective power to do work is highly developed. Herein alone lies the solution of your personal problem. In case you are loyal to nothing, your

246

existence as a private individual will remain
to you a mysterious burden, which you may
learn to tolerate, or even, if you are lucky and
thoughtless, to enjoy, but which you can never
discover to be anything of rational meaning
unless you take yourself to be a centre of
activity of which some spiritual power to which
you are loyally devoted makes use. And
this power must be much bigger and worthier
than your private fortunes, taken by themselves, can ever become. If such a spiritual
power, such a cause, such a god stronger than
you are, enters you, possesses you, uses you,
and finds you its willingly loyal instrument,
then you, just as you, have an office, a function,
a place, a status, a right, in the world. This
your right will become manifest to you only
through your loyal deeds. You will work
in the spirit of your cause. Your powers will
be dedicated to the cause, and the otherwise
miserable natural accident that there you are,
with just your sensations, your ideas, and
your physical organism, will become trans-
formed into a notable event in the great world,

— the event that precisely your unique service of your chosen cause has come to pass by your own will.

Loyalty, then, — the general spirit of loyalty, I now mean, — is a common good of mankind. It is the only good the possession of which makes any man's being thoroughly worth while from his own more rational point of view. Now, if this be so, loyalty, taken in its universal meaning, is just as much a true good in the world when my neighbor possesses it as when I possess it. If once I am wide-awake enough to grasp this fact, I shall value my neighbor's loyalty just as highly as I do my own. He indeed will be loyal to his cause, I to mine. Our causes may be very diverse, but our spirit will be one. And so the very essence of *my* spirit of loyalty will demand that I state my principle thus: *Be loyal, and be in such wise loyal that, whatever your own cause, you remain loyal to loyalty.* That is, so choose your cause, and so serve it, that, as a result of your activity, there shall be more of this common good of loyalty in the world than there would have been, had you not lived and acted. Let your loyalty be such loyalty as helps your neighbor to be loyal. Despite the diversity of the individual causes — the families, countries, professions, friendships — to which you and your neighbor are loyal, so act that the devotion of each shall respect and aid the other's loyalty.

This simpler statement of the true meaning of the principle of loyalty enables us at once to see that, when in the past loyalty has led men into crimes, — that is, into needless hostility to other people's loyalty, — it has done so, not because the men were loyal, but because they were blind to what their own loyalty signified. If they loved loyalty for its own sake (and this they did in case they were indeed loyal), then they valued loyalty not as their private possession, but for its own dear sake, as a type of spiritual activity, as a sort of human interest, that makes human life morally worth while for any man who shares this spirit. If they had remembered this fact, and if they had seen what the fact meant, they would have respected in their neighbors' lives every form of genuine loyalty, wherever they met with it. And then they would have seen that the spirit of our true loyalty is never opposed to the existence of our neighbor's loyalty. Charity, benevolence, and — simplest of all — plain fair play are tendencies that are thus to be ethically defined and deduced from our central principle. All such virtues are expressions of that loyalty to loyalty which I have now defined as the genuine and enlightened incorporation of the loyal spirit. Wherever a soldier has honored the heroism and devotion of his enemy, this honor, if it has taken practical form, has been an instance of loyalty to loyalty. One soldier fights for one cause, the other for the other. But each may, even as warrior, respect his opponent's loyalty. Let the spirit of this loyalty to loyalty spread amongst us, and it will, indeed, in no wise mean that we shall all individually serve the same causes. We must have our various causes, just as we have our various families. And no man's loyalty ought to consist wholly in a devotion to the same causes that other men serve. Loyalty is, for each man, something personal, individual. And yet, as I insist, the spirit of loyalty is a common good for all men. Each man must solve his own problem of life by means of his own form of loyalty. But the one cause that we shall all have in common will be the cause of loyalty to loyalty; that is, we shall all be disposed to make all men more loyal. Every man's individual devotion to his own cause will be just his own, but his example of loyalty, his eagerness to be the instrument of his own cause, will be a help and not a hindrance to his neighbors in the fostering of their individual form of the loyal spirit. Let this spirit of loyalty to loyalty grow amongst us, I say, and then we shall, indeed, rejoice in the loyalty of foreigners to their own nations instead of despising them for having the wrong country to dwell in. Let this spirit of loyalty to loyalty become universal, and then wars will cease; for then the nations, without indeed lapsing into any merely international mass,

will so respect each the loyalty of the others
that aggression will come to seem inhuman.
And instead of war there will then remain
only the sort of cheerful rivalry amongst our
various forms of loyalty which at present
is finely represented by good sport when fair
play prevails. For in true sport one's loyalty
to one's own side exists as immediately expressed in deeds which fully respect the opponent's loyalty to his own side, and which
involve that loyalty to the rules of the game,
and so to the common loyalty of both the opposing sides, which constitutes fair play.

III

Thus, if you please, I have sketched for you
the basis of a moral philosophy. The rational
solution of moral problems rests on the principle: *Be loyal.* This principle, properly
understood, involves two consequences. The
first is this: Have a cause, choose a cause,
give yourself over to that cause actively,
devotedly, whole-heartedly, practically. Let
this cause be something social, serviceable,

requiring loyal devotion. Let this cause, or
system of causes, constitute a life work. Let
the cause possess your senses, your attention,
your muscles, — all your powers, so long as
you are indeed active and awake at all. See
that you do not rest in any mere sentiment of
devotion to the cause. Act out your loyalty.
Loyalty exists in the form of deeds done by
the willing and devoted instrument of his
chosen cause. This is the first consequence of
the commandment: *Be loyal.* The second
consequence is like unto the first. It is this:
Be loyal to loyalty. That is, regard your
neighbor's loyalty as something sacred. Do
nothing to make him less loyal. Never de-
spise him for his loyalty, however little you
care for the cause that he chooses. If your
cause and his cause come into some inevitable
conflict, so that you indeed have to contend
with him, fight, if your loyalty requires you to
do so; but in your bitterest warfare fight only
against what the opponent does. Thwart his
acts where he justly should be thwarted; but
do all this in the very cause of loyalty itself,

and never do anything to make your neighbor disloyal. Never do anything to encourage him in any form of disloyalty; in other words, never war against his loyalty. From these consequences of my central principle follow, as I maintain, all those propositions about the special duties of life which can be reasonably defined and defended. Justice, kindliness, chivalry, charity, — these are all of them forms of loyalty to loyalty.

Even while I have set forth this sketch of a general ethical doctrine, I have intentionally illustrated my views by some references to your professional work. But at this point I next have briefly to emphasize the positive relations which physical education may have and should have to the training of the loyal spirit. Here I shall simply repeat what others, more expert than I am, have long since, in various speech, set forth.

The first way in which systematic physical training of all grades and at all ages may be of positive service in a moral education is this: Loyalty, as we have seen, means a willing and thoroughgoing devotion of the whole active self to a chosen cause or to a chosen system of causes. But such devotion, as we have also seen, is a motor process. One must be in control of one's powers, or one has no self to give to one's cause. One must get a personality in order to be able to surrender this personality to anything. And since physical training actually has that relation to the culture of the will which your leaders so generally emphasize, while some physical expression of one's personality is an essential accompaniment of the existence of every human personality, — for both of these reasons, I say, the training of physical strength and skill is one important preparation for a moral life. There is indeed a great deal else in moral training besides what physical training supplies; but the physical training can be a powerful auxiliary. Here I come upon ground that is familiar to all of you, and that I need not attempt to cover anew with suggestions of my own. The positive relation of good physical training to the formation of

a sound will is known to all of you. The only
relatively new aspect of this familiar region
that may have been brought to light by the
foregoing considerations is this: Loyalty,
as you see, on its highest levels involves the
same general mental features which are present whenever a physical activity, at once strenuous and skilful, is going on. As a skilful
and difficult physical exercise demands that
one should keep his head in the midst of
efforts that, by reason of the strain, or of the
excitement, — by reason of the very magnitude and fascination of the task, would confuse the untrained man, and make him lose
a sense of what he was trying to do, even so
the work of the effectively loyal person is
always one which requires that he should
stand in presence of undertakings large enough
to threaten to cloud his judgment and to crush
his self-control, while his loyalty still demands that he also should keep his head despite
the strain, and should retain steady control
of his personality, even in order to devote it
to the cause. Loyalty means hard work

in the presence of serious responsibilities.
The danger of such work is closely similar
to the danger of losing one's head in a difficult
physical activity. One is devoting the self
to the cause. The cause must be vast. For
its very vastness is part of what gives it worth.
I cannot be loyal to what requires of me no
effort. But the consciousness of the vastness
and difficulty of one's cause tends to crush the
self of the person who is trying to be loyal.
And a self crushed into a loss of self-possession,
a self no longer aware of its powers, a self
that has lost sight of its true contrast with
the objects about it, has no longer left the
powers which it can devote to any cause.
Mere good-will is no substitute for trained self-
possession either in physical or in moral
activities. And self-possession is a necessary
condition for self-devotion. When the apostle
compared the moral work of the saints to the
running of a race, his metaphors were therefore chosen because of this perfectly definite
analogy between the devotion of the trained
organism to its physical task and the devotion

of the moral self to its cause. In both classes of cases, in loyal devotion and in skilful and strenuous physical exercise, similar mental problems have to be solved. One has to keep the self in sight in order to surrender it anew, through each deed, to the task in hand. Meanwhile, since the task is centred upon something outside of the self, and is a serious and an imposing task, it involves a tendency to strain, to excitement, to a loss of a due self-possession, to disturbance of the equilibrium of consciousness. The result is likely to be, unless one is in a state of physical or of moral training, just a primary confusion of self-consciousness accompanied by fear or by a sense of helplessness. Against such a mood the mere sentiment of devotion is no safeguard. To hold on to one's self at the moment of the greatest strain, to retain clearness, even when confronted by tasks too large to be carried out as one wishes, to persist doggedly despite defeats, to give up all mere self-will and yet to retain full self-control, — these are requirements which, as I suppose, appear to the consciousness of the athlete and to the consciousness of the moral hero in decidedly analogous ways. And in both cases the processes involved are psycho-physical as well as psychical, and are subject to the general laws of physiology and of psychology.

Hence, when the teacher of physical training regards his work as a preparation of his pupils for the moral life, he can and should take account and take advantage of these analogies. His art is indeed one only amongst the many arts that contribute to moral training. But he may well insist that the organic virtues that he aims to establish in the bodily activities of his pupils are not only analogous to the moral virtues, but, in the loyal, may form a literal part of those virtues, since virtue exists either in action or in those results of training which prepare us for right action. To say all this implies no exaggeration of the importance of such physical education as is actually given at the present time. The whole question is one, not of inevitable or of fatal results, but of the good work that may be done, and of an alliance of the motives of physical and of moral training such as may take place if the teacher of physical training is alive to the higher possibilities of his calling.

IV

The second way in which physical training may serve the purposes of moral training is a more direct way. It is the one which Dr. Luther Gulick had in mind when he lately asserted in a paper in the *School Review* that "athletics are primarily social and moral in their nature." Dr. Gulick is well known to you as one of the protagonists in the cause of the moral importance of physical education; and you know his main argument. Social training, in boys about twelve years of age, naturally takes the form of the training which gangs of boys give to their members. A gang of boys with nothing significant to do may become more or less of a menace to the general social order. A gang of boys duly organized into athletic teams, in the service of schools, and of other expressions of wholesome com-

munity activity, will become centres for training in certain types of loyalty. And this
training may extend its influence to large
bodies of boys who, as spectators of games or
as schoolmates, are more or less influenced
by the athletic spirit. *Mutatis mutandis*,
the same considerations apply to the socially
organizing forces that belong to college athletics. The plans of those who are engaged
in physical education may therefore well be
guided, from the first, by a disposition to prepare young people to appreciate and to take
part in such group activities as these. Thus
both the physiological and the intellectual
aspects of physical training would appear to
be subordinate, after all, to the social, and in
this way to the moral, aspects of the profession.
In speaking of these moral aspects, one would
not even emphasize, as much as many do, the
central significance of the self-denial, of the
personal restraints and sacrifices, of the morally advantageous physical habits, which attend athletic training. One would rather
more centrally emphasize the view that

athletic work is not merely a preparation for loyalty, but that in case of the life of the organized athletic teams, and in case of any physical training class of pupils who work together, the athletic work *is* loyalty itself, — loyalty in simple forms, but in forms which appeal to the natural enthusiasm of youth, which are adapted to the boyish and later to the adolescent phases of evolution, and which are a positive training for the very tasks which adult loyalty exemplifies; namely, the tasks that imply the devotion of a man's whole power to an office that takes him out of his private self and into the great world of real social life. The social forms of physical training in classes or in teams require, and so tend to train, loyalty.

Physical training may then be so guided as to be a direct training in social loyalty. Your secretary has kindly put into my hands, during my preparation of this paper, two German monographs [1] whose authors insist, in some-

[1] Lorenz, *Wehrkraft und Jugenderziehung*, Voigtländer's Verlag in Leipzig, 1899; Koch, *Die Erziehung zum Mute durch Turnen, Spiel, und Sport*, Berlin, 1900.

what contrasting ways, upon this directly important office of the teacher of physical training as a teacher of loyalty and upon the value of play, of systematic gymnastics, and of athletic sports, as a training school for loyal citizenship. Both of these monographs are written under the influence of the spirit of militarism, one of them especially so; and you know now why I should view militarism as a decidedly blind, although often very sincere and intense, form of loyalty, — a form which will vanish from the earth whenever men come to an enlightened sense of what loyalty to loyalty implies. But one has to use, for the best, such types of loyalty as now prosper amongst men; and the good side of militarism is indeed the devotion that goes with it, even as the bad side of militarism is due to its implied suspicion that the loyalty of the foreigners to their country's cause is somehow in essential opposition to our own loyalty. This suspicion is false. It breeds wars, and is essentially stupid. But loyalty is loyalty still, even when blind; and I prefer blind loyalty to the sort of thoughtless individualism which is loyal to nothing. In any case our two authors are right in insisting that loyalty and physical training are closely linked by ties which ought to be recognized by those who are planning and conducting the general system of national education. So much, then, for the second positive relation of physical education to the cause of general morality. Here, again, it is true that physical education can furnish only a portion, and a decidedly limited portion, of the means and motives whereby true loyalty is trained in the young, and whereby it may also be supported in older minds. But teachers who engage in your profession have a good right to insist upon this direct social significance of their work. They do well to insist also that they can and do train such direct loyalty, not only in the work of athletic teams, but in successful class-work of all kinds, such as the teachers of physical training can direct.

V

The third positive relation of physical training to moral training is suggested by what I have said about the need of an enlightened form of loyalty. Merely blind loyalty may do mischief: but it does so, we have said, not because it is loyalty, but because it is blind. It turns into enlightened loyalty in so far as it reaches the stage of loyalty to loyalty, — the stage where one certainly does not tend merely to take over into one's own life and directly to adopt the special cause that one's neighbor has happened to choose as his own, but where one regards the spirit of loyalty, the willingness to devote the self to some cause, as a precious common moral good of mankind, — a good that we can indeed foster in our neighbors even when their individual causes are not our own, or are even, by accident, opposed to our own. I can respect, can honor, I can help, my neighbor's family loyalty without in the least wishing to become a member of his family. And just so I can be loyal to any aspect of my neighbor's loyalty without accepting his special cause as my own. He may be devoted to what I cannot and will not view as my individual cause; and still, in dealing with him, I can be loyal to his loyalty.

Now I have already pointed out that the spirit of loyalty to loyalty is finely exemplified by the spirit of fair play in games. For true fair play does not merely mean conformity to a set of rules which chance this season to govern a certain game. Fair play depends upon essentially respecting one's opponent just because of his loyalty to his own side. It means a tendency to enjoy, to admire, to applaud, to love, to further that loyalty of his at the very moment when I keenly want and clearly intend to thwart his individual deeds, and to win this game, if I can. Now in the complications of real life it is hard to keep the spirit of loyalty to loyalty always alive. If my passions are aroused and if I hate a man, it is far too easy to think that even his faithful dog must be a mean cur, in order to be able to be so devoted to his master as he is. And real life often thus confuses our judgment through stirring our passions. But it is a very precious thing when you can keep your head so clearly as to be able to oppose even to the very death, if needs must be, your enemy's cause, even while you are able to love his loyalty to that cause, and to honor his followers for their devotion to their leader, and his friends for their fidelity to him.

Now it is just such loyalty to loyalty that can be trained in true sport very much more readily than in real life, because, in sport, the social situation is simple. And because the spirit of fair play, in an athletic sport, can constantly express itself by definite physical deeds, and because the passions aroused by wholesome athletic contests ought never to be as blind, as violent, or as enduring as those which real life unhappily so often fosters, the training in fair play ought to be much easier in the world of athletic sports than the training of loyalty to loyalty is in our daily life, — much easier, much simpler, and much more definite. Hence, if games were in all cases rightly conducted, if confusing passions were properly kept from unnecessary interference with the joyous devotion of the players to their respective sides, if the general physical training of all those who are to engage in school and in college sports were conducted from the first by teachers who had a serious interest in the moral welfare of their classes, — well, if these conditions were realized, physical education ought to contribute its important share to what we have now seen to be the very crown of human virtue; namely, to the spirit of loyalty to loyalty, — to the spirit that honors and respects one's very enemies for their devotion to the very causes that one assails. The result should be the spiritual power to appreciate that common good for which even those who are mutually most hostile are contending. We human beings cannot agree as to the choice of our individual causes. We can learn to honor one another's loyalty.

The spirit of fair play, as trained in such sports as are founded upon a systematic physi-

cal and moral preparation for the strains of
contest, ought then to be made a fine preparation for the very highest and hardest
forms of loyalty, as such loyalty is needed for
the great world's social work. The spirit of
fair play, as applied in the larger social life,
has been called of late by a rather poor, if
popularly effective name, — the now familiar
name "the square deal." The name is poor,
despite the intent of the distinguished moralist
who is responsible for its recent popular usage,
because it is a name derived from games of
chance, and because it suggests that the
true spirit of loyalty to loyalty is sufficiently
shown when you merely avoid any interference with your opponent's agreed right to his
share of the chances of the game. But true
loyalty to loyalty involves a spirit that goes
much further than this. It involves an active
and effective positive respect, — yes, love,
for loyalty, wherever you meet with it, even if
the loyalty that you honor inspires those very
deeds of the opponent which you most are
required by your own cause to thwart. Now

this active and practical honor for the loyalty
of your opponents is no mere external orna-
ment of the chivalrous virtues. It is simply
the very essence of all the highest virtues.
Higher civilization depends upon it. True
justice, which certainly involves very much
more than "the square deal," true charity,
truthfulness, humanity, — these are all the
embodiments of loyalty to loyalty. And in
real life this form of virtue is at once the most
valuable and the hardest.

Here, then, is an opportunity for the teacher
engaged in physical training to set before his
pupils the highest of human ideals in an extremely practical way, and in close connection
with definite physical activities. If a man is
loyal to the loyalty that he has seen, — has
seen expressed in the activities of the play-
ground, the gymnasium, and the athletic field,
— he ought to be helped toward that loyalty
to unseen loyalty which constitutes the soul
of rectitude in great business enterprises, the
heart of honor in our national and international enterprises.

And yet this great opportunity, which the teacher of physical training possesses, is, as I need not say, attended by great and insidious dangers. Do the modern sports of our intercollegiate and interscholastic teams uniformly tend toward the encouragement of loyalty to loyalty? Is not this great moral opportunity of physical education far too much wasted, through the accidents and the excesses of our present educational system? To ask this question is to remind you of numerous recent controversies whose grave significance you all know. Great opportunities do not necessarily mean great successes. The corruption of the best may prove to be the worst.

VI

And with these words I am indeed brought to the central problem amongst all those with which this discussion is concerned. I have set forth the three sorts of positively helpful relations that a sound physical training can develop in its bearing upon the work of moral training. First, because skilful and

271

serious physical exercise involves true devotion, a sound physical training can help to prepare the organism and the personality for loyal types of activity. Secondly, physical training, in so far as it is a part of the life of a social group, can more directly aid the individual to learn to be loyal to his group. Thirdly, physical training, in so far as it can be used to give expression to the spirit of fair play, may be an aid toward the highest types of morality; namely, to those which embody that spirit of loyalty to loyalty which is destined, we hope, some day to bring to pass the spiritual union of all mankind. I have pointed out that all these three forms are simply possible forms in which the moral usefulness of physical training may appear. There is nothing that fatally secures the attainment of any of these three results. All depends upon the spirit, the skill, and the opportunities of the teacher, and upon the awakening of the right spirit in the learners. Instead of these good results, a failure to reach any of these three sorts of good results, in any tangible form, is in case of any given pupil or class of pupils perfectly possible. And, as we have just seen, the failure of certain forms of athletic sports to further, in certain well-known cases, the high cause of loyalty to loyalty has of late been far too conspicuous. Can one who approaches this topic from the ethical side suggest to you any way in which you may hope, as a body, to do more than has yet been done to make physical education morally serviceable? To this question I venture, as I close, to suggest very fragmentary answers.

In judging of the practical ideals that people cherish regarding their calling and regarding its results, one may make use of a tentative method which is likely to be at least partially enlightening. We all of us have had, in our lives, what may be called our typical great experiences, — our moments when life reached for the time its highest expression, the maxima of our curve of existence. Poets love to talk about such moments; romancers dwell upon them in narrating their stories; our own memories glow when we recall our own moments of this general type. A conversion or a sudden relief from great sorrow, a homecoming, the reunion of lovers long parted, the moment of hearing the first cry of some newborn infant, — these are familiar instances of what may be such maxima in the curve of experience of this or of that human being, — glorious discoveries of new success or of great attainment. Well, our personal and our professional activities, our avocations and our vocations, our exercises and our sports, are characterized each by its own type of maximal experiences. And you can tell something about the moral character and the deeper significance either of a person or of an occupation when you hear some typical report about what was, from the point of view of this person or of this occupation, the type of experience which seemed, in its own place and setting, to have such a maximal character.

It has occurred to me to suggest, as one way of estimating the moral value of those experiences which one person or another may associate with athletic activities, an examination

of some of the reports that experts, who also
happen to be authors, have given of what to
their minds seemed to be the truly great moments of athletic activity, — the moments when
one most deeply experiences what, to himself
personally, the whole business in the end
means. Of course our daily life has to be lived,
whatever our profession, upon a somewhat
commonplace level. And it is upon such levels
that, after all, we have to win many of the
best moral results that devotion can bring into
our lives. But just as love is for a lifetime,
but the stories of love's triumphs centre about
the exaltations of the moment when two souls
first find each the other, so it is our general
custom to conceive the moral values of every-
day life in terms of our memory or imagination
of the great instants of life.

> " Then felt I like some watcher of the skies
>   When a new planet swims into his ken; "

says Keats; and one knows at once to what
sort of exaltation he refers. *This* maximum
of experience stands for a type of consciousness in terms of which the poet conceives all

the long hours and days through which he devoted himself to Chapman's Homer.

Well, I have asked myself, how do expert athletes conceive the maximal moments of their lives as athletes? With what exultation are they filled when they contemplate their greatest attainments? Tell me that, and I can do something to comprehend their moral attitude toward their work, and the perils and the uses of this attitude.

Of course, any one who tells, in an expert way, a story of athletic triumphs, will depict, in lively fashion, the moment of victory. And, of course, the exultation of victory, taken by itself, has somewhat uniform characters, such as any boys' story of sports or any lively newspaper picture of a great game will portray. I need not dwell upon the fact that victory in any contest is keenly joyous, and constitutes a maximum point in the curve of experience, and that whoever writes a lively sporting story keeps you in suspense for a time, as the spectators at the game are kept in suspense, and then thrills you with the elemental delight of the victorious solution of the problem of contest, as the cheerful romancer lets the lovers agonize awhile, and then indeed somehow startles you with the perfectly familiar thrill of discovering that their hour of joy at length arrives. Such incidents are æsthetically attractive; but they are not the sorts of maximal experiences that I now have most in mind. For my present purpose, I want to know whether, as the expert recalls the moment of his highest athletic attainment, he thinks of anything besides victory, and whether this other feature, besides victory, which at such great instants he has before him, and which he later recalls, is of the nature of a morally significant enlargement or fulfilment of any higher self, so that the memory of this maximum is indeed any sort of moral inspiration in later life.

Let me quote to you at once the report of an expert, in which he tells of a great athletic experience of his own, associated, as it was, with no little peril. In the year 1896 Philip Stanley Abbot, a Harvard graduate of the class of 1890, was killed by an accident during an attempted ascent of Mt. Lefroy, in the Selkirks. He was a man of great intellectual promise and power, and an experienced and devoted mountain climber, whose death left mourning a very wide circle of friends. In a memorial of Abbot that was published in the annual report of the Sierra Club of California, there is printed a passage from a letter which he once wrote to a friend about his first Selkirk expedition, — an expedition antedating by some time the final and fatal attempt to ascend Mt. Lefroy. The passage has the interest that Abbot, who was a scholar and a moralist, as well as a mountain expert, had long found in his mountain climbing a moral inspiration, which aided him in the hard work of his practical life. He was no pleasure-seeker and no boaster. He had chosen his Alpine avocation because he found in it a moral support that, to his mind, justified its peril. Was his judgment sound in this particular? Well, let him tell his own tale: —

"Palmer's old theory, that the nearest approach that we can make toward defining

the *summum bonum* is to call it 'fulness of
life,' explains a great many things to me.
Once we came out at seven o'clock upon the
crest of a snow mountain, with two thousand
feet of rather difficult snow work before
us, when I had expected plain sailing, — and
the daylight had already begun to fade. At
the bottom of the two thousand feet we were,
as it proved, still five miles from home; but we
could have camped there. But where we were
there was nothing more level than the roof of
a house, except the invisible bottom of an
occasional huge crevasse, half masked and
half revealed. I had been feeling lifeless all
that day, and we had already had nine hours
of work. But the memory of that next hour
is one of the keenest and most unmixed
pleasures I have carried away, — letting one's
self go where the way was clear, trusting to
heels alone, but keeping the ice-axe ready for
the least slip, — twisting to and fro to dodge
the crevasses, planning and carrying out at the
same instant, — creeping across the snow-
bridges like snails, and going down the plain

slopes almost by leaps, — alive to the finger-
tips, — is a sensation one can't communicate
by words, but you need not try to convince me
that it isn't primary. However, this by the
way."

You will all recognize this, I take it, as a
maximal experience of a type that belongs
to what one might call the lucid athletic
activities, wherein the highest exertion, the
completest devotion of the self to the end in
hand, are accompanied by the clearest sense of
the social relation to one's fellow-workers, and
so by the fullest self-assertion, self-expression,
or, as Abbot calls it, by the fulness of life.

Now are all the great sports equally characterized by such lucid self-possession at the
maximal moments, — by such complete union
of the active self and its object that skill,
devotion, and success are all equally clear
facts of consciousness just when the loftiest
height of the experience is reached? That
is a technical question which I have no right
to try to answer upon my own authority.
But, when I turn to the ordinary sporting

story, I find that the highest height is said to be reached, in the mental life of some sports, just when, amidst the plaudits of vast crowds, in the intoxication of relief from suspense, in the exhaustion of the completely worked out organism, — when, I say, at such an instant, — the higher centres refuse to function definitely, and the victorious hero turns into an automatic physical mechanism, that somehow, half consciously or unconsciously, accomplishes in a blind way the crowning deed of triumph, while a sort of aurora of glorious and confusedly blessed sensations flickers dizzily and massively in the place where the hero's mind had before seemed to dwell. In a recent sketch by Mr. Ruhl, "Left Behind," the success of the hero in a mile foot-race culminates in a kindly but subconscious automatism on the hero's part, whereby he turns at the moment of winning, catches in his arms his fainting and defeated rival as the latter crosses the line, and carries him, then, to the tent near by. What followed, while the hero worked to revive his prostrate fellow-contestant, is thus depicted: "Outside the crowd cheered and howled, and pushed up against the canvas walls, and from the distance came the boom of the band, marching to them across the field. He [the hero working to revive the defeated rival] swabbed on witch hazel desperately — panting, dizzy with excitement and happiness, and a queer happy-weepy remorse. The Other Man opened his eyes and blinked.

"'Bill,' he grinned the best he could, and held out his hand, 'I guess we've been fools long enough.' Then he got tired again. 'It was a great race,' he said, without opening his eyes. The hero replies, 'Yes! yes.' He meant," continues our author, "that he thought it had been long enough. Somehow he couldn't remember any words. And then the crowd came in."

Now contrast these two maximal moments of athletic experience: in the one, the self alive to the finger-tips with devotion and triumph, joyously laboring side by side with its comrades amidst the beautiful and merci-

less fields of snow, and just above the half
visible depths of the crevasses; in the other,
the self with its "queer happy-weepy remorse,"
confused, automatic, kindly, but maudlin.
These are, I say, two maximal experiences,
each to be remembered for a lifetime. Each
has its obvious physical and psychological
conditions. Each is quite in order in its own
context. I have, of course, no objection to
offer to the existence of either of them, when
it comes to the man who has earned it and
who has his right to it. But the contrast
suggests at once a fair question. On the
whole, since we are prone to estimate our lives
and our daily work so much in terms of
such maximal experiences, let us ask then
which forms of sport, other things being
equal, are, on the whole, likely to be best
adapted to the steadiest sort of moral training, — those whose highest heights are
reached in a state of "happy-weepy remorse," amid howling crowds and dizzy
confusions of consciousness, or those sports
whose loftiest hours or moments of triumph

leave the self "alive to the finger-tips," not with mere muscular sensations, but with the sense of clearly conscious devotion, of self-possession, and of exalted, yes, genuinely spiritual, mastery of something that, however hard or perilous, seems to be worth mastering. All kinds of sport have, no doubt, their functions. I am, as you see, venturing to answer here no technical questions; nor do I doubt that there are maximal moments in the lives of all of us when we are, in Shelley's phrase, "dizzy, lost, yet unbewailing." Yet, on the whole, I can venture to say that, educationally considered, and especially from the point of view of moral education, those forms of sport must be best whose highest moments leave one as clearly in possession of himself, and of his loyal relations to his mates and his rivals, as the physical exhaustions attending these highest moments permit.

Now this word about the experiences attending sport is meant here simply to make definite this closing suggestion regarding the conditions that must aid in keeping either a set of class exercises in gymnastics or a sport upon a high level as a means of moral education. What your athletic exercises need, in order that they may attain a high grade of moral efficacy, is a set of social conditions such as tend to clear-headedness rather than to confusion, such as at their highest point shall lead to Abbot's and Professor Palmer's fulness of life rather than to the flood of "happy-weepy remorse" or of other enjoyable destructions of moral equilibrium. For loyalty means clear-headedness; and you all regard sound wits, skilful and definite activities, lucidity, as mental traits that are to be trained by the greater part of all those class exercises and all those sports that you yourselves most admire. The evils, however, of the recent school and college sports have resulted, so far as I can see, almost wholly from the unsound social conditions which have been allowed to surround and to attend both the intercollegiate and the interscholastic games. For the ethics of sport have come, through the recent social conditions, to be influenced, both directly and

indirectly, by the confused and unprincipled
sentiments of great crowds of people, and, in
general, by the intrusion of enthusiasms
whose origin is due to the fact that too many
people have been interfering in mass, in
thoughtless ways, through the press, or through
the presence of excited and cheering multitudes,
— have been interfering with the moral education of our youth. Nobody can learn loyalty
from mobs. The Harvard Stadium is an
admirable place when it is not too full of
people. But when it is full of people it is a
bad place for the moral education of our
athletic youth, just because, by the size of the
crowds that it collects, it encourages, even in
the most highly trained men and even in the
most intelligent and skilful of sports, ideals
that inevitably centre far too much about those
poorer sorts of maximal experiences to which
I have made reference and too little about
that type of fulness of life which Philip
Abbot glorified. Every athletic reform at
Harvard must aim to minimize not so much the
athletic as the social perils of modern sport.

But you, the teachers engaged in physical education, are fostering the sort of athletic life that flourishes in small, clearly defined, well-organized social groups. Whether class work or games are made prominent in this or in that part of your teaching, you are all working to combine in your pupils skill, devotion, loyalty of the individual to his community, and, whenever you have an opportunity to insist upon fair play in difficult situations, you are teaching loyalty to loyalty.

My purpose in this paper has been to suggest the correlation of your work with that of others who are engaged in moral education. Loyalty to the community and loyalty to loyalty, — and both of them expressed, not in confused sentiments, but through clearly conscious deeds, — these are the traits that the teacher of morals must inculcate. You see the task. I have suggested its dangers. I am sure that you, "alive to the fingertips," are ready for your share of the perils of our great modern educational effort to find our way to the high places of the Spirit.